Contents

Editor's Introduction

'The essence of our lawyer's craft lies in skills ...; in practical, effective, persuasive, inventive skills for getting things done ...'

Karl Llewellyn

The appearance of this new series of texts on legal skills reflects the recent shift in emphasis in legal education away from a focus on teaching legal information and towards the teaching and learning of task-related and problem-solving skills.

Legal education in the United Kingdom has undergone significant changes over the past ten years as a result of growing concern, expressed for the most part by the profession, over its adequacy to prepare students for the practice of law. At the same time, many legal educators have voiced fears that concentrating on drilling students in substantive law promotes neither the agility of mind nor the development of judgment skills which provide the basis for continued learning.

Today courses providing clinical experience and instruction in legal skills are increasingly a part of undergraduate law programmes. Both branches of the profession in England and Wales have fundamentally revised the content and format of their qualifying courses to include direct instruction in practical skills. In Scotland, the Diploma in Legal Practice, which emphasises the learning of practical skills, has been in place since 1980/81.

Nonetheless, legal skills education in the United Kingdom is still in its infancy. Much is to be learned from other jurisdictions which have a longer history of the use of practical and experience-based teaching methods, lessons invaluable to UK law teachers many of whom now face the challenge of developing new courses on legal skills. The ready exchange of ideas between skills teachers in the United Kingdom and abroad is an important part of the development process. So too is the generation of 'home-grown' texts and materials designed specifically for legal skills education in undergraduate and professional schools in the United Kingdom.

The introduction of skills teaching into the legal education curriculum has implications not only for what students learn in law school but also for how they learn. Similarly it has implications for the kind of textbooks which will be genuinely useful to students who wish to succeed in these programmes.

This new series of texts seeks to meet this need. Each text leads the reader through a stage-by-stage model of the development of a particular legal skill; from planning, through implementation in a variety of guises, to evaluation of performance. Each contains numerous practical exercises and guides to improve practice. Each draws on a network of theories about effective legal practice and relates theory to practice where that is useful and relevant.

The authors are all skills teachers with many years of practical experience at all levels of legal education. They draw on relevant literature and practice from all over the common law world. However each book is written specifically for students of law and legal practice in the United Kingdom and sets learning in the context of English law and against the backdrop of the Law Society's standards for the new Legal Practice Courses, due to commence in 1993/4.

Each of these texts is designed for use either as a supplement to a legal skills course taught at an undergraduate or professional level, or as a model for the structure and content of the course itself. We recommend the use of these books, therefore, to students and skills teachers alike, and hope that you enjoy them.

Julie Macfarlane
London, Ontario
January 1993

Legal education in the United Kingdom has undergone, if not a transformation, a substantial change in recent years. Along has come the realisation (at least to many) that students should, and can, acquire skills as well as knowledge.

This text is dedicated to the students and staff who shared the inaugural year of the Postgraduate Certificate in Laws at the City Polytechnic of Hong Kong, not the least of whom was Julie Macfarlane.

David Stott
April 1993

Acknowledgements

I am grateful to Jo for being patient, to Julie for being unusually so and for making so many useful comments on the manuscript, to Diana for permission to use her LEXIS exercises, to David and Kathy for their support and to Linda. I would also like to thank my Research Module students for their tolerance in being used yet again as guinea pigs and particularly David Harper for permission to use selected extracts from his research assignment.

David Stott
April 1993

CHAPTER

1 Introduction

'Every book must be chewed to get out its juice'

Chinese proverb

1.1 Legal research and legal knowledge

This text is concerned with the skill of legal research. Effective legal research is central to the lawyer's role as problem-solver.

Undergraduate legal education exposes students to a large body of legal rules. As an undergraduate you may well spend, or have spent, a large part of your life committing these rules to memory. Any system dominated by the traditional unseen examination as a form of assessment must demand that you memorise large amounts of written detail so that you can, hopefully, demonstrate a knowledge of the rules as they then existed. A great deal of this, of course, is wasted energy. Many of the laws you once religiously memorised are no more. In many cases, the law has moved on.

1.2 So what do you already know about legal research?

What will be of continuing and lasting value to you in legal practice, however, will be your acquired knowledge of how the law works; in other words, an understanding of the principles which underlie the operation of the law and the legal system. These include the sources of law and the relationship between these sources, the operation of judicial precedent, the principles of equity and of statutory interpretation. At another level these principles must also include an understanding of the relationship between the judiciary and other organs of government, the various influences (political, economic and social) on judicial decision-making, the impact of the adversarial system of trial on law and law-making and the relationship between domestic and international law, in particular EC law. If you understand these principles and their various relationships you are already part of the way to being an effective legal researcher.

It is likely that you will have received some formal instruction on how to research a legal problem as part of the traditional 'induction course' at the beginning of your undergraduate programme. This may have been rather cursory and you may have little memory of it. You may have received more in-depth instruction on legal research, though the expectation is often that this is something you will 'pick up' for yourself. Undoubtedly, you will have acquired some legal research expertise while an undergraduate, in particular if you have prepared extended pieces of coursework or a dissertation. Yet it remains a common complaint from the professions that the research skills of trainee solicitors and pupil barristers are far from developed. The claim is sometimes made by graduates themselves that it is possible to obtain a law degree without even seeing the inside of a law library!

1.3   How this book can help

Legal research is a complex skill. As a practitioner, you will need to be familiar with at least those areas of the law in which you claim to have expertise. This means that you must be able to find the law in those areas and to update your knowledge constantly. You must also be able to plan your research in order to make best use of available time and resources. You will need to be thorough, and you will also sometimes need to be creative; real-life problems are rarely text book problems. This book can help you to develop all these skills and to become a more effective legal researcher.

1.4   Monitoring your progress

Written standards have now been articulated for the skills components of the Legal Practice Course. For legal research, they are as follows:

'The student should understand the need for thorough investigation of factual and legal issues and should understand the need for preparation and the best way to undertake it.

The student should be able to:

- a) determine the objectives of the lawyer or client
- b) identify and analyse factual material
- c) identify the legal context in which factual issues arise
- d) identify sources for investigating relevant facts
- e) determine when further facts are required
- f) identify and analyse legal issues
- g) apply relevant legal provisions to facts
- h) relate the central legal and factual issues to each other
- i) identify the legal, factual and other issues presented by documents
- j) analyse a client's instructions and be able to identify the legal, factual and other issues presented by them
- k) present the results of research in a clear, useful and reliable form.

The student should be able to demonstrate an understanding of:

- i) the use of primary and secondary texts
- ii) the methods of locating cases and statutes
- iii) the use of treatises, periodicals, digests, and standard practitioner texts
- iv) the use of indexes and citators
- v) the use of computerised research tools.'

Whether you are an undergraduate student or a student on a professional course, you may find it helpful to use these standards as a benchmark for your progress as you work through this book.

1.5   A three-stage model for legal research

Effective legal research may be regarded as a three stage process: research planning; research implementation; and the presentation of research findings. It is important that you are able to plan your research strategy in advance, to avoid wasting time in the law library. You can then use this plan to access primary and secondary sources with confidence. The results of your research, outlined in your final presentation, will reflect the efficiency with which you undertake these first two steps. Each of these three stages of research require a variety of sub-skills as illustrated below:

1.5.1   Research planning

a) fact collection

b) legal knowledge

c) problem identification

d) legal analysis

e) fact analysis

f)   further fact collection

g) identification of avenues of research

h) generation of key search words

1.5.2   Research implementation

a) identification of problem(s) for resolution

b) identification of relevant source materials

c) location of source materials

d) effective use of source materials

e) analysis of research findings

f) application of findings to problem(s)

g) identification of further problems

1.5.3   Research presentation

a) identification of the recipient's (client's or principal's) needs or requirements

b) selection of appropriate format eg letter, memorandum, report, brief

c) use of clear and succinct language

d) use of appropriate language style eg informatory, advisory, recommendatory, demanding

The aim of this text is to give you advice on how you might proceed in each of these stages in conducting your future legal research tasks. It is not intended to be prescriptive but to encourage you to think about your existing research practices and how you can experiment and improve upon them. The text is practical in approach and involves you actively, by providing you with numerous opportunities for research exercises. You are invited to compare your products with those of the author. You are strongly recommended to use these opportunities for practice and not to move directly to the sample products. Each section of the text - whether on research planning, implementation or the presentation of research findings - is worked around a particular area, or areas, of common legal practice and thus draws on areas of substantive law which form part of both undergraduate LLB programmes and the Legal Practice Course.

CHAPTER

2 Research Planning

'The outcome of any serious research can only be to make two questions grow where only one grew before.'

Thorstein Bunde Veblen (1857-1929)

2.1 Why plan?

Think back to a time when you were required to research a legal topic, perhaps a piece of coursework or a dissertation, perhaps a moot or a debate. What did you do? How did you go about it? Did you avoid research in primary sources and rely on the available secondary sources in the form of text and case books? Did you rush straight to the law library and desperately search the available indexes for any and all information on a given subject? Did you seek the librarian's help in a state of panic? Alternatively, did you sit down and plan your research task carefully? Did you clarify exactly what it was you needed to find out? Did you identify possible alternative ways of accomplishing your research task? Did you select the most effective?

If the former sounds familiar, it is likely that you habitually obtain the information you want by operating a 'blanket bombing' approach. As you were probably aware at the time, such a method is seriously inefficient.

This chapter is concerned with the preliminary organisation of effective and efficient research, that is, research planning. The importance of pre-planning the time you will spend accessing primary and secondary sources cannot be over-estimated. If you plan your research properly, you will save yourself and your client time and money, and can guarantee results which are pertinent.

As a practitioner, it is unlikely that you will be confronted on a daily basis with broad and abstruse academic issues. You will be confronted with specific problems of a practical nature. You will need to identify exactly what the problem is and then proceed in a focused way to identify alternative possible resolutions. This chapter will propose:

- that you review and evaluate your existing practices of research planning
- that you experiment with and evaluate alternative systematic techniques to assist you in the identification and analysis of material facts
- that you experiment with and evaluate alternative techniques of creative thinking to assist you in analysing the material facts and legal issues ascertained, and in identifying alternative resolutions
- that you practice generating effective and alternative search terms for research purposes.

2.2   Steps in research planning

The following steps in research planning will be considered:

- fact collection
- fact analysis (and identification of relevant legal principles)
- identification of factual and legal issues
- formulating a research plan

In this chapter, the fact pattern is drawn from the area of civil litigation and involves a personal injuries claim.

2.3   Collect the facts

Your first task as a lawyer will be to collect all relevant facts from all possible sources. Your legal knowledge will assist you in seeking and identifying relevant facts.

You will have engaged in this process at undergraduate level although the likelihood is that, in formulating problems, your tutors will have selected the relevant facts for you. However, you have read legal judgments and will appreciate that, before a decision can be made on the law, the judges engage in a process of fact extraction or selection. You may also have been confronted with this task yourself if you have been required to read a transcript of a case, rather than a reported case with a headnote.

2.4   Fact collection exercise

Consider the following brief fact situation related by your client, Robert Tee, aged 17, in an initial interview.

Robert seeks your advice on seeking compensation for injuries he suffered in a road accident.

On June 3, 1992, Robert left school at approximately 4.00 pm on his moped, which he had bought second-hand. He was wearing a crash helmet. He had, at that time, been driving the moped for some 2-3 months and held a provisional licence. While driving home, Robert was involved in an accident with a car. It later turned out that the driver of the car was Eileen Moriarty, a middle-aged woman and librarian by profession. Eileen was taking her aged aunt, Noreen, back to a local old people's home after an afternoon's outing. Robert has no memory of the accident or of the events immediately preceding it. He knows that the shoe to his right foot was subsequently found in the car. A local resident, Maureen Bell, heard the collision, telephoned the police, and went to Robert's aid. Ms Moriarty and her aunt remained in the car which was on the right-hand side of the road. Robert was severely injured. A policeman and an ambulance arrived at the scene of the accident. Robert was hospitalised for 6 weeks, during which time he underwent a series of operations, in particular for injuries to his right leg. He has been left with a slight limp, a number of scars on the right leg, thigh and left arm, and regular debilitating headaches. For the time being, he has had to give up his Saturday job. He was unable to take a holiday in Europe with his girlfriend which had been booked for July. He will probably not be able to return to school for the September term and, if so, may have to defer taking his 'A' levels. He has received conditional university offers for October 1993, but will be unable to take these up should he defer his 'A' levels. In any case, he is no longer confident of achieving the required grades because he becomes tired very easily and the headaches are regular and severe. Robert was a keen sportsman and had been hoping to complete his Duke of Edinburgh Gold Award in the coming academic year. Robert has been interviewed by the police and understands that the driver of the car is to be prosecuted.

2.4.1   Exercise One

Spend 5 to 10 minutes itemising the known material facts from the account of Robert Tee's accident and any further facts which you think you will need to know together with the sources from which you will find them.

How did you set about this task? Did you adopt a systematic and ordered approach or list material and further facts and potential sources as they came into your head?

Each of these methods has its value. The systematic application of a series of questions is more likely to ensure that your final list does not contain serious omissions. 'Brainstorming' - listing all the possibilities which come into your head without first evaluating them - may lead to more creative thinking but may be more appropriate to the later stage of *fact analysis* (see below at 2.5) and dispute resolution rather than *fact collection*. Creative techniques are of limited value in establishing what the facts are but may be productive in identifying fact omissions.

Very simple methods can assist in the compilation of systematic lists of necessary facts. Try using the systematic method outlined below and compare the results with those achieved by conducting a brainstorming exercise. This method uses a series of monosyllabic questions in relation to each of the parties.

The plaintiff

WHO?
WHAT?
WHEN?
WHERE?
WHY?
HOW?

The defendant

WHO?
WHAT?
WHEN?
WHERE?
WHY?
HOW?

Your initial source of information is likely, of course, to be your client. You can use these questions as 'prompters' to remind you to ask the essential questions in initial interview. Using this systematic method would lead to the acquisition of the following basic information in the case of Robert Tee:

The plaintiff

WHO?   Robert Tee of 10 The Drive, Dewsbury, West Yorkshire. Aged 17. A pupil at Batley Grammar School.

WHAT?   An accident in which a car collided with Robert's moped causing him serious injury.

WHEN?   On 3 June 1992 at approximately 4.00 pm.

WHERE?   Outside 15 Dewsbury Road, Batley, West Yorkshire.

WHY?   Due to the alleged negligent driving of the defendant.

HOW?   The defendant's car left the left-hand side of the road without reason and collided with Robert's oncoming moped.

Having collected the primary facts from your client, you will have a basic idea of the nature of the problem and, hopefully, will be able to identify the relevant area of law. You can now move on to amplify these facts and to identify further facts by talking with your client. Omissions of factual detail can also be identified, and the sources from which these facts can be obtained. Your knowledge of the law will assist you in asking questions which will elicit further relevant information.

On some occasions you may be required to deal with problems outside your existing range of knowledge and expertise. Using this simple technique will still assist you in gathering relevant facts, though it is likely that you will gather a number of irrelevant facts also.

2.4.2   Exercise Two

Before moving to the next section, spend 5 to 10 minutes identifying what further questions - possibly using the headings suggested above - you would ask of Robert Tee and why.

You have already learned that Robert has sustained injuries in a road accident due to the alleged negligence of a car driver. The area of law is one with which you are familiar: the tort of negligence. It appears from the preliminary facts that Robert has a potential cause of action against the driver. The case is worth pursuing. You will not be wasting your time or your client's. But there are many further facts which you need to learn from your client, some of which will be prompted by your knowledge of the law of negligence:

WHO

- is the defendant?
- is acting for the defendant?
- are the witnesses?

WHAT

- was the speed limit?
- speed was Robert driving at?
- speed was the defendant driving at?
- were the weather conditions?
- physical injuries did Robert sustain?

WHO

- was the police officer called to the scene of the accident?

WHAT

- action are the police taking?

WHO

- treated Robert's injuries?

WHAT

- damage was done to Robert's moped?
- other loss did Robert sustain?
- are Robert's goals in pursuing an action?

WHY

- did the accident occur? Was there fault on Robert's part? Did Robert need to wear glasses when driving? Was Robert an experienced driver? Does Robert have any convictions for motoring offences?
- were Robert's injuries so extensive? Was Robert wearing a crash helmet?

By now, you will have a fairly detailed factual account of the event. Some of this information may need to be verified or followed up.

2.4.3   Exercise Three

Now spend 5 to 10 minutes working through the above list and the list you generated for yourself and identify possible follow-up actions.

Your list might include:

- enquiries of the police to obtain the accident report, statements from the parties and witnesses
- if the police report does not disclose the weather conditions on the day of the accident, you may wish to make enquiries of a meteorological office
- enquiries of the consultant to obtain confirmation of the injuries sustained by Robert and a prognosis for his recovery
- enquiries of the headmaster/mistress of the school to confirm Robert's predicted 'A' level grades and the delay in the taking of his examinations
- enquiries of Robert's optician as to the extent of his visual disability

Once you have obtained the results of your follow-up enquiries, your fact collection should be complete - at least for the time being. But examine your new facts carefully; they may give rise to the necessity for further fact investigation.

2.5   Analyse the facts

Once you have gathered your facts you will be in a position to analyse their significance. You will have undertaken some fact analysis already in extracting or selecting the facts you consider to be of relevance. Again there are simple techniques available to assist you in a systematic process of fact analysis.

2.5.1   Example One

The following is a technique known as West's system. It suggests that you next analyse your data under the following heads:

Parties

Objects

Places

Basis

Defence

Relief

• **Parties**

Under this head, you are required to identify the *status* of the parties to the action in terms of either their relationship to each other or as individuals. For example, the relationship between the parties may be one of landlord and tenant, husband and wife, licensee and licensor, employer and employee, doctor and patient, central government and local government, promissor and promissee etc. One of the parties may have a particular status or characteristic; for example, as a minor, trespasser, government official, bankrupt, alien, policeman. This status may well be a significant factor in the application of the law. Further, identifying the parties' status or special characteristics will assist you in identifying the relevant area of law and legally significant aspects of the case. In our example, you would only be able to identify the status of Robert as a minor (in itself, not relevant) and describe him as the victim of a road accident who has suffered injury. However, the latter will be sufficient to guide you to the law of tort and road traffic and you will also be reminded when you conduct your research to determine whether Robert's status as a minor is a material fact.

• **Objects**

Under this head, you are required to analyse the significance of the objects identified in the fact situation. In our example, the objects involved are (i) a car (ii) a moped (iii) a missing crash helmet (iv) a pair of glasses. Each of these objects can be described at various levels of specificity/generality. The car could be described as a Renault or a vehicle; the crash helmet as protective clothing; the glasses as indicating a disability. It is important when analysing the objects identified that you identify them in both broad and specific terms. You are here generating key words for research. When undertaking your research, you are unlikely to find case-law or statutory authority which refers specifically to Renault cars or glasses. On the other hand, you are likely to find authority which refers specifically to crash-helmets.

- **Places**

The place where the event took place may be of legal significance and therefore is worthy of analysis. Was it public or private, domestic or commercial, in a place of employment, on premises to which one was invited? In our example, the location of the accident might be significant. Was it in a built up area, at a junction, at traffic lights, on a blind bend? Was part of the road obstructed by, for example, road works or a fallen tree?

- **Basis and Defence**

This involves the legal basis on which the action will be founded and potential defences thereto. In our example, the basis of the action will clearly be the duty of care owed by one road user to another in the law of negligence, whether there has been a breach of that duty and consequent damage. You will recall the possible defences to such an action as including *novus actus interveniens*, remoteness and contributory negligence. The main defence in our example is likely to be based on contributory negligence.

- **Relief**

Here you are concerned with what your client wants and what the law allows him to have. It is important that you explore what your client's wishes and preferences are and do not make assumptions. In the case of a purchase of faulty goods, for example, does your client want a refund, the goods to be exchanged for a new or different model, the goods to be repaired, compensation for the inconvenience, or the shop where the goods were purchased closed down? In our example, it is likely that Robert's main objective is to be compensated for his injuries and other losses suffered as a consequence of the accident. He may want to protect others from the same fate and so want to ensure that the car driver is disqualified from driving. He may want revenge!

2.5.2   Example Two

As an alternative to West's system, you may use 'brainstorming', which is a far less structured approach to fact analysis. Brainstorming is at its most effective when operated by a group of people. Once familiarised with the facts, the group addresses one or a series of questions in turn. Here, one broad question might be: 'Does Robert have a claim in the law of tort?' Each member of the group then calls out a word or phrase to describe any issue which comes to mind. These are noted for future discussion and evaluation. The group does not interrupt the brainstorming process to consider the relevance or merits of individual group member's contributions, or to call for further information or elucidation. The whole essence of brainstorming is that it demands immediate, instinctive and intuitive responses. Once the brainstorming session is exhausted (3-5 minutes) the group proceeds to discuss each of the contributions. The adoption of this method might produce a list such as the following which the group then proceeds to elucidate, organise and analyse:

negligence

tort

duty of care

breach

fault

liability

accident

date

limitation period

damage

foreseeability

injury

prognosis

prosecution

liability

helmet

contributory negligence

glasses

road conditions

driver

Road Traffic Acts

visibility

witnesses

police reports

2.5.3   Example Three

Another method of fact analysis is 'mind-mapping'. Here, in diagrammatic form, the analyst identifies a central theme or proposition and then branches out from that proposition to identify facts (and fact omissions) and inferences which support or deny the central theme. An example for the case of Robert Tee is illustrated in Diagram I. Please note that this method can also be used for the identification of factual and legal issues.

It will be clear by now that fact collection and analysis is inextricably bound up with identification and analysis of the relevant law. Without a basic knowledge of the law, you cannot begin to distinguish relevant from irrelevant facts. Without proper and full identification of the relevant facts, you cannot hope to identify the specific relevant legal principles for analysis and application. In particular, you will not be in a position to recognise facts which might help you - or your opponents - to apply or distinguish existing authorities.

Diagram I
Mind mapping

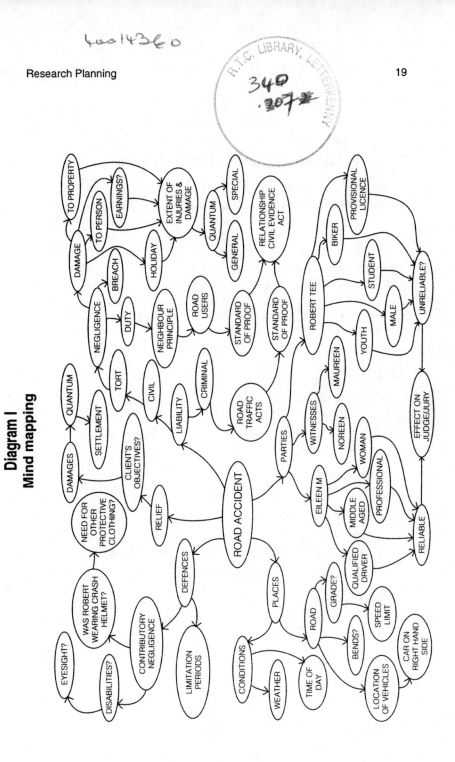

2.6   Identification of factual and legal issues

Once you have gathered your facts and, so far as possible at this
stage, distinguished the relevant from the irrelevant, you will be in
a position to organise them and, in so doing, to relate the facts to
the relevant legal principles and vice versa. Organising the factual
information you have obtained so far will assist you in identifying
the factual and legal issues and focus the subsequent steps in
your research plan. A chronological organisation of information
may be adequate, though this is unlikely unless you simply want a
record of events at the initial stage of your investigation. A
number of possible approaches to organising your factual data
are suggested below.

2.6.1   Example One

You could next organise your facts under the following heads,
identifying any special facts and asking yourself the following
questions (some of this information you could take directly from
your West's system chart, above at para 2.5.1).

- **Causes of action**

  Identify the main legal basis of the action and the facts
  which support your client's case.

  Are there facts which may obstruct your client's case? Are
  there any barriers to activating the cause of action?

  Are there any alternative courses of action, legal or non-legal?

- **Special facts**

  Identify facts, if any, which may serve to distinguish your
  client's claim from existing authority.

  Is the distinction to your client's advantage?

- **Defence**

  Identify potential defences which might be raised.

  What facts support these defences?

- **Special facts**

  Identify facts, if any, which may serve to distinguish the potential defences from existing authority.

  Is the distinction to your client's advantage?

- **Relief**

  Identify what potential relief your client might obtain.

  Are there any barriers to relief being granted?

- **Threshold issues**

  Identify any fact which may dispose of the case (eg has a statutory limitation period already expired?).

  Are there facts which make it very undesirable or unnecessary to proceed?

  Are there facts which are conclusive to the outcome of the case?

Exercise Four

Before reading further, spend 10 minutes completing a planning chart in this format for the case of Robert Tee.

2.6.2   Example Two

Alternatively, you can formulate what are known as preliminary issue statements, that is, statements of the research questions you need to address. These can be prioritised in accordance with their importance or 'threshold' value (eg does the basis of your client's case depend on one particular question which must be answered first?). The purpose of preliminary issue statements is to assist you in identifying the relevant law, the questions which raise legal issues and the legally significant facts by addressing the heads 'under', 'did' and 'when'. For instance, in our example:

Preliminary issue statement 1

> **under** the tort of negligence
>
> **did** Ms Moriarty breach her duty of care as a road-user
>
> **when** she collided with Robert Tee in a built up area when travelling at excessive speed in broad daylight with good weather conditions

Preliminary issue statement 2

> **under** the tort of negligence
>
> **did** Robert contribute to his injuries
>
> **when** he failed to wear his glasses when driving

Preliminary issue statement 3

> **under** the Limitation Acts
>
> **did** Robert institute proceedings in time
>
> **when** the accident occurred on 3 June 1992

2.6.3   Example Three

Another approach to relating the facts you have already identified to the relevant legal principles, is to take the information you have obtained and transfer it onto a chart on five levels of analysis, as illustrated overleaf (Diagram II).

This chart effectively demonstrates the interdependence between law and fact discussed earlier in this chapter. It has been used on professional legal training programmes in a number of common law countries as an aid to the rigorous analysis of law and fact and the subsequent identification of legal and factual issues. It also appears as a tool for analysis in the 'Advocacy' text in this series (by Andy Boon). It can be explained as follows:

Level 1   The lawyer first must research the law thoroughly to ascertain with precision the place in the body of the law where the 'source' of the client's 'right' is contained.

Level 2   She must then translate that right into a stated 'cause of action' and identify the particular jurisdiction in which that cause of action can be sustained. At this level also the lawyer considers 'parties'. Who is the appropriate plaintiff/defendant?

Level 3   The lawyer then knows that to succeed in the litigation she must establish with precision the matters which require proof in a cause of action of that kind. These matters are commonly called the 'ingredients' of the cause of action or, in a criminal case, the 'elements' of the charge.

Only after establishing a framework of this kind can the lawyer proceed to Levels 4 and 5.

Level 4   These are those propositions of fact which support each of the Level 3 'elements' of the case.

Level 5   Each proposition of fact (Level 4) must in turn be supported by evidence admissible in court whether physical, witness testimony or other.

Diagram II

Charting Levels of Analysis

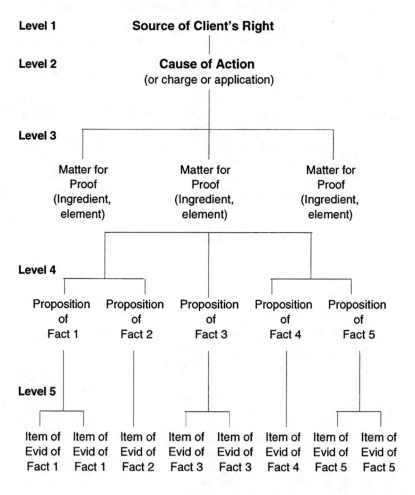

Level 1   **Source of Client's Right**

Level 2   **Cause of Action**
                      (or charge or application)

Level 3

Matter for	Matter for	Matter for
Proof	Proof	Proof
(Ingredient,	(Ingredient,	(Ingredient,
element)	element)	element)

Level 4

Proposition	Proposition	Proposition	Proposition	Proposition
of	of	of	of	of
Fact 1	Fact 2	Fact 3	Fact 4	Fact 5

Level 5

Item of	Item of	Item of	Item of	Item of	Item of	Item of	Item of
Evid of	Evid of	Evid of	Evid of	Evid of	Evid of	Evid of	Evid of
Fact 1	Fact 1	Fact 2	Fact 3	Fact 3	Fact 4	Fact 5	Fact 5

Source: Institute of Professional Legal Studies, New Zealand

Exercise Five

Before reading further, spend 15 to 20 minutes using this method for our case study.

You might have produced something similar to the following, or possibly something more complex:

Level 1

Source of client's right: the law of tort

Level 2

Cause of action: use of the civil law of negligence by the injured party

Level 3

Matters for proof:

   i) that Eileen Moriarty, as driver of the car, owed a duty of care to Robert as a fellow road user;

   ii) that Eileen breached the duty of care;

   iii) that Robert suffered damage as a consequence;

   iv) that there was no intervening act (*novus actus interveniens*);

   v) that Robert had not contributed to his injuries by way of contributory negligence.

Level 4

Propositions of fact:

   i) duty of care

      a) that Eileen was the driver of the car;

      b) that the car was involved in a collision with a moped;

      c) that Robert was the driver of the moped.

   ii) breach of duty

      d) that Eileen was driving negligently;

      e) that Eileen's lack of care caused the accident.

iii) damage

    f)   that Robert suffered physical injuries;

    g)   that Robert suffered financial loss.

Level 5

Evidence to support propositions (a) - (g) above:

  (a)

    i)   the car was registered in Eileen's name;

    ii)   Eileen is the only named driver on her insurance;

    iii)   Eileen was in the driver's seat when the policeman arrived at the scene of the accident;

    iv)   the only other person in the car was Eileen's aunt who cannot drive.

  (b)

    i)   the car and moped were both in a damaged state;

    ii)   after the accident, the car and moped were located within 50 feet of each other;

    iii)   traces of paint were found on the moped which matched with the colour of the car;

    iv)   when Maureen Bell appeared on the scene shortly after the accident, there was no other vehicle on the road;

    v)   when the car was examined by the policeman, a boy's shoe was found inside.

  (c)

    i)   Robert was found unconscious in the vicinity of the accident;

    ii)   there was no other injured party in the vicinity;

    iii)   Robert had a missing a shoe.

(d)

   i)   skid marks leading to where Eileen's vehicle stopped indicate that she was travelling in excess of the speed limit;

   ii)   Eileen has since been prosecuted and found guilty of driving without due care and attention.

(e)

   i)   does *res ipsa loquitur* apply?

(f)

   i)   a report from Dr Bentham of Batley General Hospital which confirms that Robert suffered fractures to the right femur, right fibia, right clavicle and left thumb and lacerations to the right knee, right heel, right lower leg, face and forearm, an immediate loss of consciousness and subsequent throbbing headaches;

   ii)   a prognosis from Robert's consultant.

(g)

   i)   Robert's insurance papers show the purchase price of the moped and date of purchase;

   ii)   correspondence from Robert's motor insurance company confirms that the moped was written off and that the company agreed to pay £360 to Robert in satisfaction of his claim;

   iii)   Robert's insurance certificate shows that he was liable for a £50 excess;

   iv)   correspondence from the travel company confirms that Robert had a holiday booked for July and that he lost his deposit as a result of cancellation;

   v)   receipts from Robert's parents show that immediately after the accident he received treatment as a private patient and these detail the costs incurred.

By utilising the information you have obtained from one or more of the above methods, you will now, hopefully, have a complete account of the facts, actual and inferred, to date. You should have identified the relevant area of law to be researched and, most importantly, the specific questions to be resolved by your research.

2.6.4   Generation of key words or search terms

To assist you in conducting your research you will need to generate a list of key words, that is, alternative words or phrases which might be used in indexes and bibliographies. The importance of developing an accurate and creative list of key words and phrases to use in all index searches cannot be over-estimated. The level of generality or specificity of your search terms will depend on the index or bibliography you are planning to use. If an index of texts, for example, your search terms will be broadly formulated and you should try to think of as many synonyms as possible. If you are planning to use LEXIS or another legal index then your search terms are likely to be much more specific. See Chapter Five for a more detailed discussion of generating search terms for LEXIS use.

Exercise Six

Generate a list of search terms which might assist your research in the case of Robert Tee.

2.7   Summary

In this chapter, we have considered the importance of systematic planning as a preliminary step in conducting legal research. The better prepared you are, the more likely it is that your research implementation and outcomes will be efficient and effective. There is no one set routine of planning for research. What this chapter tries to do is to suggest a series of methods which can be utilised individually or collectively to assist you at the planning stage of legal research. You may adopt these methods in formulating your research plan or adapt them. You should ultimately develop your own personal method of research planning. The method itself is less important than the end result - an effective plan which saves you time later in your research task.

An outline for a research plan is given at the end of this chapter. You are advised to experiment with this when planning for research and to analyse the product. Was the plan effective in assisting you to collect and identify relevant facts and omissions and legal issues which needed further research? Which of the methods worked most effectively for you and why?

Of course, planning for research takes time and, when under pressure, you may feel inclined to adopt old habits and minimise the time you devote to planning and preparation. This is, however, likely to prove bad time management in the long run. If your research is inadequately planned, your research product is likely to be incomplete, if not inaccurate. If you - or your principal - can identify weaknesses in your product, then you will have to spend at least as much time plugging the holes. If you fail to do so, you will not be providing a complete service to your client.

You are now ready to move on to the next stage of your research - in the law library.

Sample research plan

1 Collect the facts

WHO?
WHAT?
WHEN?
WHERE?
WHY?
HOW?

2 Analyse the facts

PARTIES
PLACES
OBJECTS
BASIS
DEFENCE
RELIEF

or try brainstorming?

3 Identify factual and legal issues

CAUSES OF ACTION
SPECIAL FACTS
DEFENCE
SPECIAL FACTS
RELIEF
THRESHOLD ISSUES

4 Formulate preliminary issue statements

PRELIMINARY ISSUE STATEMENT 1
UNDER

DID

WHEN |

PRELIMINARY ISSUE STATEMENT 2
UNDER

DID

WHEN |

or try drawing a mind map to illustrate the factual and legal issues?

5 Chart levels of analysis

LEVEL 1

LEVEL 2

LEVEL 3

LEVEL 4

LEVEL 5

6 Generate a list of search terms

1
2
3
4

7 Identify research sources (complete this section after you have read Chapter 3)

1
2
3
4

2.8   End of chapter references and additional reading

Ramsfield, J   *Getting it Right and Getting it Written*
(1989)   West Publishing Co

Wren, C and Wren, J   *The Legal Research Manual*
(1986)   West Publishing Co

CHAPTER

3   In the Law Library

'We received clear evidence from both the College of
Law and the Council of Legal Education that some
students arrived at the vocational schools exhibiting ...
an inability to undertake independent legal research.'

Marre Committee Report 1988

3.1   From planning to practice

As an undergraduate, you may have become familiar with the
information retrieval services available in your law library.
Although much of the research necessary to deliver up-to-date
information will have been done for you by your tutors, you should
have found it necessary on occasions to extend and up-date that
information for yourself. However, undergraduates vary
enormously in the extent to which they develop library-based
research skills during their degree studies. Many, for whatever
reason, become very largely dependent on the use of secondary
source materials such as text books and do not realise the need
to locate and explore primary sources in the form of cases,
statutes and statutory instruments, and European legislation.

If you are still an undergraduate, you should aim to develop
efficient library-based research skills. These will be invaluable to
you both now and in the future. As a trainee, you will no longer be
able to avoid legal research. You will not be able to refer
constantly to your principal for answers as you may have referred
in the past to your tutors. Your principal will be expecting you to
find and up-date the law as necessary for the resolution of the
problem at hand.

This chapter is concerned with establishing how much you
already know about standard library-based information retrieval
systems, and with developing your existing skills in order to use

those resources effectively. It will deal in particular with accessing and up-dating the law with reference to a particular case or statute or by subject matter.

There are many other resources to which reference will not be made in the space of this chapter. There are now excellent texts on the market to which you might refer for a more detailed account of how to use a law library. The primary objective of this chapter is to ensure that you can put your research plan (see Chapter 2) into practice by accessing the major sources of case-law, statutes and statutory instruments.

The resource materials considered here should be found in your university law library. The next chapter will consider library resources which are of particular relevance to the practitioner and of which you will have gained little, if any, familiarity in your undergraduate studies.

This chapter aims to:

1   review and evaluate your existing knowledge of and ability to use the standard library-based legal information retrieval systems;

2   enable you to utilise such systems appropriately and effectively in finding and up-dating the law.

You will find a number of exercises in this chapter on the use of the standard legal bibliographies. It is essential that you attempt these in order to become familiar with how each resource operates. Sometimes you are provided with a method and answer. Sometimes a question is posed without a given answer. On these occasions, it may be helpful to compare both your answer and your method of reaching it with a colleague.

Finally, because the variety of possible sources may seem bewildering until you have become familiar with the advantages and disadvantages of each, two sections - a 'Quick Find Checklist', and 'Why to use What, and When' - are included at the end of this chapter which suggest how to best use the various indexes.

3.2   Exercise One: Diagnostics

You will find below a summary of the facts of the well-known case of *Jeffrey v Black* [1978] QB 490. Read the questions and identify how you would locate the primary sources necessary to answer each of them. Then test the accuracy of your answers in the law library. This is an individual exercise. You are expected not to consult with others nor to seek the assistance of the librarian.

> Black was having a drink in a pub which was known to be frequented by drug dealers and users. He had not eaten that day and, being short of cash, he stole a sandwich from the bar while the barman was not looking. Unfortunately, the pub was under surveillance by two plain-clothes police officers who had observed Black's actions. They arrested Black for theft and took him to the police station. Without Black's permission, the officers went to his home and searched it. They found a quantity of drugs. Black was charged with being in possession of prohibited drugs.

Two main issues are raised here:

* the legality of the search of Black's home
* the admissibility of the drugs as evidence at his trial.

Questions

1 Where would you find alternative citations for *Jeffrey v Black*?

2 How would you identify in which, if any, cases *Jeffrey v Black* has been (a) applied (b) distinguished (c) followed or (d) overruled?

3 Where would you look for the full text of the provisions of the Police and Criminal Evidence Act which cover (a) the legality of searches of premises and (b) the admissibility of evidence unlawfully obtained?

4 Where would you locate cases decided on the relevant provisions of the Police and Criminal Evidence Act?

5 How would you find out whether the relevant provisions of the Police and Criminal Act are still in force?

6   How would you locate articles written on (a) the legality of searches and (b) the admissibility of evidence illegally obtained?

7   Where would you find a statement of the current legal position on each of these issues?

If you can identify an appropriate resource to answer each of the above questions immediately and if reference to these resources in the law library leads you to the answers, you obviously have a basic ability to use the standard legal bibliographies and can use this chapter to consolidate and extend your knowledge. If not, you should read the following pages with great care. They will give you a guide to the main legal bibliographies with diagrams to illustrate their use. You might then attempt the above questions again.

You are advised to read the remainder of this chapter in your law library and to cross-refer constantly to the bibliographical service being reviewed.

3.3   Current law

The Current Law Services, published by Sweet & Maxwell, provide comprehensive coverage of legal developments since 1947. Until 1991 a separate Service operated for Scotland. The Service is constantly up-dated, accessible and user-friendly. Current Law Services provide:

•   Case and Legislation (formerly Statute) Citators

•   Monthly Digests

•   Weekly Reviews

•   Year Books

•   Statutes Annotated

•   European Current Law

The Citators provide quick reference guides to case-law, statutes and statutory instruments.

3.3.1   The case citators

In cumulative volumes covering the periods 1947-76, 1977-88 and 1989-92, the Case Citators provide, in alphabetical order, a list of cases (from England, Northern Ireland, Scotland and the EC) reported or considered with citations and a full history of the cases reported to date. The Citator is issued annually. By using the Case Citator you can find:

• the full name of any case reported from 1947

• alternative citations for each case cited in the instant court and the courts below

• the names of and a citation for cases decided before 1947 but considered in cases since 1947

• if decided in a higher court, a reference to the status of the court

• a reference to the year and paragraph of the Year Book in which the case is digested. The Year Book paragraph references to cases appear in bold type. If there is no year reference then the case is contained in the consolidated volume 1947-51.

• a Year Book reference to cases in which the case cited has been applied, considered, explained, approved, not followed, reversed or overruled etc

• references to journals or periodicals in which the case cited has been considered. Such references are denoted by the use of square brackets around the reference.

The Case Citator also contains a list of abbreviations used. It is up-dated in the Monthly Digest (see below).

Using the Case Citators, you will be able to access the full history of any reported case decided since 1947 and the post-1947 history of any case judicially considered since that date. The citation for the case of *Jeffrey v Black* is shown in Diagram I.

Diagram I

Using the Current Law Case Citator

Jeffrey v Black [1978] QB 490; [1977]
3 WLR 895; (1977) 121 SJ 662; [1978]
1 All ER 555; [1977] Crim LR 555, DC.

.......*Digested*, 77/**2263**: *Applied*, 78/2568:
Followed, 85/665

You will see from Diagram I that the Case Citator gives you the following information on *Jeffrey v Black*:

• alternative citations

• a reference to the volume of the Current Law Year Book (1977) and the paragraph in that volume (2263 - in bold type) where you will find a digest of the facts and decision

• references to the volume year and paragraph number of the Year Book where you will find a digest of a case in which *Jeffrey v Black* has been applied (1978 at para 2568) and followed (1985 at para 665)

You will note from the alternative citations that sometimes the year appears in square and sometimes in round brackets. If it appears in square brackets, the year is an essential element in enabling you to find the case in that particular report. If it appears in round brackets, it is the volume number which is essential and you can locate the case without reference to the year.

The Case Citators may refer you to articles on the case cited. If so, the whole of the reference to the article will be contained in square brackets.

The Case Citators also refer to unreported decisions which have been judicially considered in later cases.

Remember that once you have located citations for the case you are seeking, you may wish to check the subsequent Case Citators to see if the case has been judicially considered. Finally, bring yourself fully up-to-date by referring to the cumulative case citator in the latest Current Law Monthly Digest. Examine the Weekly Law Reports and the Daily Law Reports to up-date from the date of issue of the Monthly Digest.

3.3.2 The legislation (formerly statute) citators

In cumulative volumes for the periods 1947-71, 1972-88 and 1989-92 and arranged chronologically by reference to year and chapter number, the Legislation Citators provide:

- a Table of Abbreviations Used

- a Table of Statutes referred to in the volume (alphabetical with year and chapter number)

- a Statute Citator for the period to which the volume applies (chronological and chapter order). The Citator covers:

    i) statutes passed in the period with the date of the Royal Assent;

    ii) statutes affected during the period by statutory instrument;

    iii) statutes of any date judicially considered during the period with relevant case names and citations;

    iv) statutes of any date repealed or amended during the period with references to the amending or repealing statute by title, year and chapter number.

Each Citator also includes a Legislation Not Yet In Force Table and a Table of Statutory Instruments Affected.

The Legislation Citator is up-dated in the Monthly Digest and the Statutes Annotated current loose-leaf service.

Diagram II

Using the Current Law Statute Citator

---

34. Planning and Compensation Act 1991.

Royal Assent, July 25, 1991.

Commencement orders: 91/2067, 2092(S), 2272, 2905

ss 3, 9, see *Doncaster Borough Council v Green, The Times, November 21, 1991, CA.*

s 84, orders 91/2067, 2092(S), 2272, 2905

sch 4, regs 91/2794

sch 18, amended: 1991, c 60, sch 1; repealed in pt: *ibid* sch 3.

You will see from Diagram II that the Statute Citator gives you the following information on the Planning and Compensation Act:

- the chapter number (34) of the Act
- the short title of the Act and the date on which the Act received the Royal Assent. This does not necessarily mean that the Act entered into force on that date.
- the commencement order(s) which bring the Act, in whole or in part, into force
- references to sections which have been judicially considered and the name(s) of the relevant cases with a citation and a reference to the status of the court. Remember that you can obtain alternative citations, if necessary, by using the Case Citators.
- references to orders made under a section(s) of the Act and regulations made under schedules to the Act

- references to amendments or repeals to the Act and to the amending or repealing statute by chapter number and section or schedule as appropriate (which you can then locate using Current Law Statutes Annotated).

Remember - if the Act is before 1947, it may still be listed in the Legislation Citator if it has been amended or repealed since 1947. In this case, you will need to check all the Statute Citators.

Exercise Two

a) Were any provisions of the Police and Criminal Evidence Act 1984 not in force as at 30 March 1992?

b) Were any provisions of the Children and Young Persons Act 1969 not in force as at 30 November 1992?

3.3.3   The Monthly Digest

The Digest is a general monthly up-dating service with sections on the law of England and Wales, the European Community (including all decisions of the European Court of Justice), Northern Ireland and Scotland. Its contents include:

- a list of UK subject headings under which material in the Digest is organised

- a section on the Law of the Month for England and Wales, the EC, Northern Ireland and Scotland. This provides, under the appropriate subject heading, summaries of cases and digests of statutory instruments and Practice Directions etc with references to articles and books published. The EC section includes digests of legislation, summaries of European Court decisions and references to articles and books published.

- a series of tables (which, where appropriate, are cumulative and contain references to cases reported to date that year) on topics such as quantum of damages and High Court fees as well as a Table of Cases, a Statute Citator and a Table of Statutory Instruments.

- a General Index arranged alphabetically within subject headings (cumulative)
- a list of law books published during the month

The Current Law Monthly Digest is invaluable as an aid to keeping abreast of developments in the law.

3.3.4   Current Law Week

This recently launched weekly bulletin provides a further up-dating service. It includes case digests, statutory instruments, practice guidance and press releases.

3.3.5   Year Books

These are annual volumes which revise and consolidate the Monthly Digests, although the Year Books for 1947-51 have been consolidated into one volume. The volumes for 1956, 1961, 1966 and 1971 are cumulative for these periods respectively. Since 1971, only the subject index has been cumulated and this is contained in the 1976 volume (for the period 1947-76) and in the 1986 volume (for the period 1972-86). The Year Books from 1986-90 are also available on CD ROM.

The arrangement of the Year Book is somewhat different from the Monthly Digest. Its contents include:

- Digest of Headings in Use
- Table of Cases with references to the Year Book by paragraph number
- Table of Statutory Instruments (arranged alphabetically, within subject headings and numerically)
- Dates of Commencement Tables - Statutes - for England and Wales, the EC, Northern Ireland and Scotland
- Indexes of articles and books published during the year (alphabetical within subject headings)
- a General Index (alphabetical within subject headings).

3.3.6   Statutes Annotated

Current Law Statutes Annotated is a loose-leaf service with annual bound volumes. The contents of each set of annual volumes includes:

- a Table of Statutes (chronological for the year)
- an Index of Short Titles (alphabetical)
- all public general Acts, private Acts and Commencement Orders. Major Acts are fully annotated, including references to Parliamentary debates and the background to the introduction of the Act.
- an Index by subject heading for the year (alphabetical by subject within subject headings) with references by chapter and section number.

The final issue of 1992 contains an alphabetical Table of Statutes from 1700 to date which is up-dated at the beginning of each year.

Diagram III

Using Current Law Statutes Service

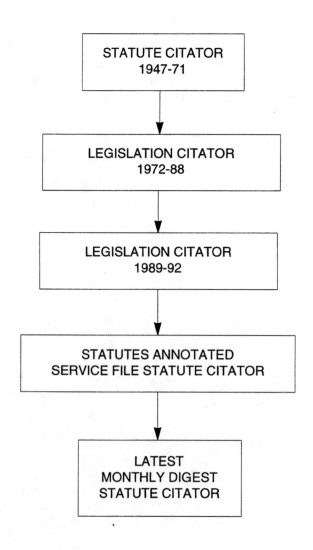

STATUTE CITATOR
1947-71

LEGISLATION CITATOR
1972-88

LEGISLATION CITATOR
1989-92

STATUTES ANNOTATED
SERVICE FILE STATUTE CITATOR

LATEST
MONTHLY DIGEST
STATUTE CITATOR

When using Statutes Annotated

- start with the Citator which covers the period in which the Act you are seeking was passed. Then check all subsequent Citators for amendments, repeal, statutory instruments issued and cases in which the statute was considered.
- if you want the full text of the Act, refer to the relevant volume of Statutes Annotated
- Statutes Annotated will provide you with the background to and a commentary on the statute
- Statutes Annotated for the immediate year past will be contained in loose-leaf volumes. Once complete for the year, these will be bound.
- always remember to up-date by reference to the Monthly Digest.

Exercise Three

Have the gaming laws relating to Bingo been amended since January 1991?

3.3.7   European Current Law Monthly Digest

This Monthly Digest, which commenced in January 1992, provides a guide to legal developments in Europe (East and West). It can be accessed by subject or country. Each Digest includes:

- a list of subject headings used in the volume
- digests of cases from the EC, European states, the Council of Europe and international organisations, arranged by subject-heading (or cross-referenced by paragraph number to where in the volume a relevant case is digested under an alternative heading)
- legislation recently passed under subject headings.

The European Current Law Year Books consolidate the Monthly Digests.

Exercise Four

When did the United Nations Charter enter into force for San Marino?

3.4   Halsbury

This service, published by Butterworths, consists of Halsbury's Laws, Halsbury's Statutes and Halsbury's Statutory Instruments and the Annual Abridgment. Butterworths also publish a companion volume of digests of case law from the UK, the Commonwealth and the EC in the form of The Digest. Using Halsbury can, at times, be somewhat perplexing but it is an essential resource and persistence will be rewarded! After first reviewing the contents of the constituent parts of the Service, this section will concentrate on clarifying how, and for what purposes, the Service may be used.

3.4.1   Halsbury's Laws of England

First published in 1907, the current edition is the 4th, completed in 1986. Halsbury's Laws provides a comprehensive statement of the law of England and Wales. Arranged in alphabetical order by subject title, it comprises:

- the Main Volumes
- a Consolidated Subject Index
- a Consolidated Table of Cases, Statutes and Statutory Instruments.

Halsbury is up-dated by:

- an Annual Cumulative Supplement
- a Monthly Review Service
- a Noter-Up.

Some Main Volumes are themselves up-dated and re-issued at intervals.

The Main Volumes

There are 52 Main Volumes in the series arranged alphabetically according to subject matter with some 165 titles. Each volume identifies on its spine the range of subjects with which it deals. Each Main Volume includes:

- a Table of Statutes (alphabetical)
- a Table of Statutory Instruments (alphabetical)
- a Table of Cases (alphabetical)
- a Table of Cases in the ECJ (chronological)

as well as a series of Tables on EEC and Euratom Regulations, Community and other Treaties and Conventions, and EEC and Euratom Decisions and Directives.

The Consolidated Subject Index

Contained in two volumes (55 and 56), the Consolidated Index is a reference for all subject titles within individual volumes.

It is possible that a Main Volume has been up-dated and re-issued since the publication of the Consolidated Index. If a volume is a re-issue it will be identified as such on the spine and the date to which the re-issue volume is current will be given at the front of the volume.

The Halsbury Service also publishes The Consolidated Tables of Statutes, Statutory Instruments and EC Materials (Vol 53) and The Consolidated Table of Cases (Vol 54).

The Annual Cumulative Supplement

This up-dates the Main Volumes to 31 October of any one year and identifies entries by reference to the relevant volume and paragraph number. New subject matter formerly outside the scope of the existing Main Volumes is identified by placing a letter pre-fix at the beginning of the relevant paragraph in the Supplement. Each Supplement supersedes the previous one and includes a

Table of Statutes and a Table of Cases (both arranged alphabetically). The Supplement also includes a Table of Decisions of the European Court of Justice (arranged numerically).

The separately published Annual Abridgment contains cases and legislation not included in the Annual Cumulative Supplement.

Halsbury's Current Service provides a loose-leaf service to ensure that the law is current. This consists of two binders, the Monthly Review (Binder 1) and the Noter-Up (Binder 2).

The Monthly Reviews include the following:

• digests of cases reported and articles published during the month under subject headings

• cases before the ECJ and legislation from the EC Council and Commission

• a Cumulative Index covering the contents of the Monthly Reviews by subject heading and alphabetically within those headings.

The Noter-Up details developments since the last Annual Cumulative Supplement. It is cumulative, organised in the same way as the Main Volumes, and issued monthly. It includes:

• Commencement of Statutes Table

• Practice Directions

• words and phrases judicially interpreted

• EC materials.

Diagram IV

Stages in Using Halsbury's Laws

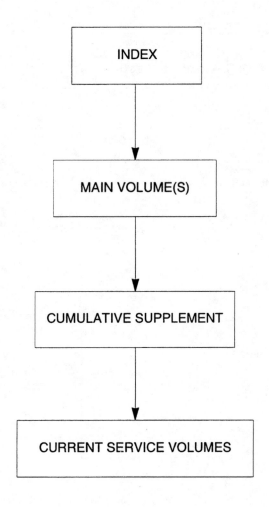

Diagram V

How to use Halsbury's Laws

to search by subject

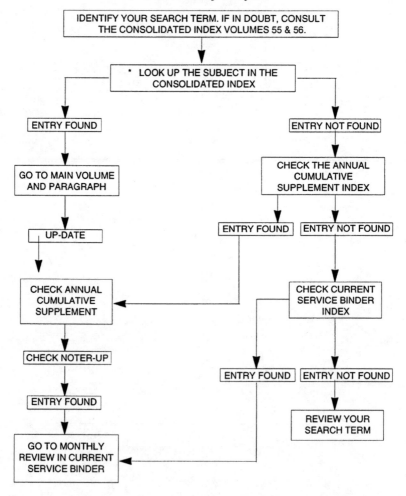

IDENTIFY YOUR SEARCH TERM. IF IN DOUBT, CONSULT
THE CONSOLIDATED INDEX VOLUMES 55 & 56.

*   LOOK UP THE SUBJECT IN THE
CONSOLIDATED INDEX

ENTRY FOUND

ENTRY NOT FOUND

GO TO MAIN VOLUME
AND PARAGRAPH

CHECK THE ANNUAL
CUMULATIVE
SUPPLEMENT INDEX

UP-DATE

ENTRY FOUND

ENTRY NOT FOUND

CHECK ANNUAL
CUMULATIVE
SUPPLEMENT

CHECK CURRENT
SERVICE BINDER
INDEX

CHECK NOTER-UP

ENTRY FOUND

ENTRY NOT FOUND

ENTRY FOUND

REVIEW YOUR
SEARCH TERM

GO TO MONTHLY
REVIEW IN CURRENT
SERVICE BINDER

*   To search by statute or case name, use the
Consolidated Tables, Volumes 53 & 54, and proceed

Notes to Diagram V

* It is possible that a Main Volume has been re-issued since the Consolidated Index or the Consolidated Tables. Whether a volume is a re-issue will be identified on the spine and the date to which the re-issue is current will be stated towards the front of that volume. If the re-issue is later than the Consolidated Index or Tables, use the re-issue index.

* Identify an appropriate search term used in the Halsbury index. Often, one of the most difficult aspects of using Halsbury is to identify the search term used. You can do this by referring to the subject titles contained in the Consolidated Index or by browsing the spines of the Main Volumes for the broad subject headings used. However, the latter strategy is risky as you might identify the wrong title. For example, a reference to the admissibility of evidence improperly obtained might be contained in either the volume on Criminal Law or the volume on Evidence.

* Always up-date. Look up the volume and paragraph number found in the Annual Cumulative Supplement and also check the Monthly Review (Binder 1) and the Noter-Up (Binder 2).

Exercise Five

Your client, Mr Gee, seeks your advice on whether he can prevent his girlfriend, who is three months pregnant, from having an abortion. Mr Gee believes he is the father of the child.

Use Halsbury's Laws to identify the relevant law (case law and statute) to enable you to advise this client.

3.4.2   Halsbury's Statutes

First published in 1929/30, the current edition is the fourth, completed in 1989. Halsbury's Statutes provides a comprehensive, annotated record of all Acts of Parliament currently in force. Arranged in alphabetical order by subject title, the service comprises:

- the Main Volumes
- the Current Statutes Service
- the Tables of Statutes and General Index (currently up to July 1992)
- Is It In Force?

Halsbury's Statutes is up-dated by an Annual Cumulative Supplement and a loose-leaf Noter-Up service and some Main Volumes are revised and re-issued at intervals.

The Main Volumes

There are 50 Main Volumes in the series arranged alphabetically according to subject matter with over 140 titles. Each volume identifies on its spine the subjects with which it deals. Each Main Volume contains:

- References and Abbreviations
- Tables of Statutes (alphabetical and chronological)
- Tables of Treaties
- Tables of Statutory Instruments appearing in the annotations to Acts in the volume
- Tables of Cases referred to in the volume
- Full text of statutes under subject headings with annotations including the background to the Act and cross-references to other primary and secondary legislation and relevant case-law

It is possible that a Main Volume has been re-issued since the Tables of Statutes and Index. Whether a volume is a re-issue will be identified on the spine and the date to which the issue is current will be stated at the front of the volume.

The Current Statutes Service

These loose-leaf volumes contain Acts published since the Main Volumes.

The Table of Statutes and General Index

This volume is a reference for all subject titles given in individual Main Volumes and the Current Statutes Service. It is arranged alphabetically and by subject. Acts which have come into force since publication of the Main Volumes will be found in the relevant Current Service Binder. These Acts are identified in the General Index by the letter (S).

The Annual Cumulative Supplement

The Supplement records changes and additions to the published Main Volumes and Current Service and contains all new Acts, statutory instruments and leading case-law on the subject topics of the Main Volumes. Each Annual Supplement replaces the previous issue.

Is It In Force?

This annual volume contains the commencement date of every public general Act passed in the last 25 years.

The Noter-Up

This loose-leaf service up-dates the current Annual Cumulative Supplement and Is It In Force?

Diagram VI
Using Halsbury's Statutes
by statute title or subject

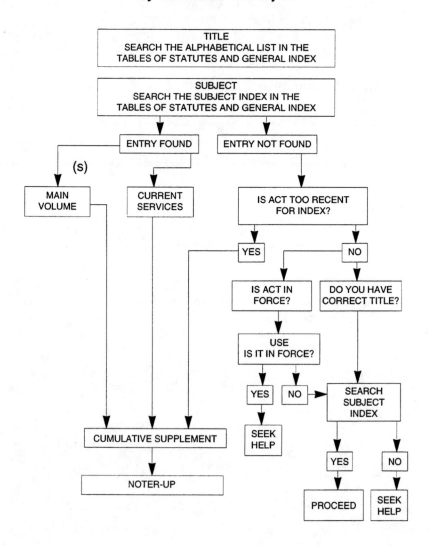

Notes to Diagram VI

- It is possible that a Main Volume has been re-issued since the Tables of Statutes and General Index. Whether a volume is a re-issue will be identified on the spine and the date to which the re-issue is current will be stated towards the front of that volume. If the re-issue is later than the General Index, use the re-issue index.

3.4.3 Halsbury's Statutory Instruments

There are 22 Main Volumes in the series arranged alphabetically according to subject matter with 97 titles. Each volume identifies on its spine the subjects with which it deals. Each Main Volume contains:

- a chronological list of instruments
- tables of instruments no longer in operation
- cross-references to other titles in the work where related instruments may be found.

In addition to the Main Volumes, you may also use the following service volumes to assist you in your research.

The **Main Service Binder** is arranged alphabetically in year groups and its contents include:

- a title key which lists subject titles with corresponding volumes
- a chronological list of instruments contained in the Main Volumes
- a table of enabling statutes under which the statutory instruments were made with the subject title under which the instrument appears
- an Annual Cumulative Supplement
- a Monthly Survey providing a monthly up-date from the issue of the latest Annual Supplement.

The **Additional Texts Binder** reprints the more important statutory instruments issued each month.

Finally, you may access the indexes to the Main Volumes and the Annual Consolidated Index.

The latter, which covers the Main Volumes and the Annual Supplement, adds new and removes superseded statutory instruments. It refers to the volume and page where the instrument can be found and gives the instrument's year and number.

Halsbury's Statutory Instruments can, therefore, be used to locate an SI by reference to title, subject, citation or the enabling Act.

3.5   The Digest

Formally titled Annotated British, Commonwealth and European Cases (formerly The English and Empire Digest), the first edition of the Digest was published in 49 volumes between 1919 and 1932. The latest edition is the third, published in 1986, totalling some 63 volumes. The Digest provides, in summary form, the whole case law of England with selected cases from Scotland, Ireland, Australia, Canada, New Zealand and other Commonwealth countries and the EC. Annotations give subsequent cases in which judicial opinion has been expressed in the English courts. It is up-dated by an Annual Cumulative Supplement and Continuation Volumes. Some Main Volumes are revised and re-issued at intervals. The service comprises the Main Volumes; the Consolidated Table of Cases; the Consolidated Index; the Annual Cumulative Supplement and Continuation Volumes.

There are over 50 Main Volumes in the series arranged by subject title with sub-headings within each title. So far as possible, the titles correspond to those used in Halsbury's Laws, with new titles being added as the need arises and out-dated ones replaced. An alphabetical list of cases will be found at the front of each volume and a list of contents at the front of each title.

Cases are summarised with citations arranged chronologically within headings and sub-headings and include references to subsequent decisions in which the case cited has been considered.

Diagram VII
Using the Digest

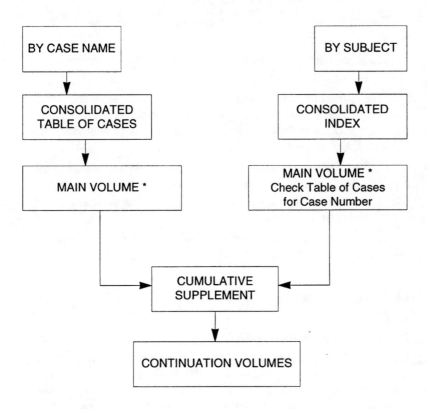

*   It is possible that a Main Volume has been re-issued since the
    Consolidated Table of Cases or Index. Whether a volume is a
    re-issue will be identified on the spine and the date to which
    the re-issue is current will be stated towards the front of that
    volume. If the re-issue is later than the Table/Index, use the
    re-issue Table/Index.

The Main Volumes of the Digest are also usefully cross-referenced to Halsbury's Laws and Halsbury's Statutes (see paras 3.4.1 and 3.4.2 above).

The Consolidated Table of Cases is an alphabetical list of cases in the Main Volumes.

The Consolidated Index is a subject index, in alphabetical order, to The Digest.

The Annual Cumulative Supplement up-dates the series with new cases, annotations and developments in the law. It contains a Table of Cases which extends the Consolidated Table of Cases. It also contains instructions on How to Use the Digest.

Finally, **Continuation Volumes** extract case digests from former Annual Supplements. When a Main Volume is re-issued, cases from the Continuation Volumes and the Supplement to date are incorporated.

The Digest can, therefore, be used to find a case either by subject or by case name.

3.6   Other indexes

3.6.1   The Legal Journals Index

The Legal Journals Index indexes articles from all legal journals published in the UK from 1986. The index is arranged under subject headings (so one article may be indexed under several headings), author, cases referred to under the name of both plaintiff and defendant and legislation referred to. It is issued monthly, with quarterly and annual cumulations. For a fee (currently £20 for 15 minutes), the editors will conduct a search for you on a particular topic and provide photocopies of articles indexed.

3.6.2   Index to Legal Periodicals

First published in 1908, this US publication indexes articles from some journals in the UK, Ireland, Canada, Australia and New Zealand. Articles are indexed alphabetically under author and subject. References to cases and statutes referred to are indexed separately. It is issued monthly with quarterly and annual supplements and triennial cumulative editions.

3.6.3   Index to Foreign Periodicals

First published in 1960, this indexes articles on international and comparative law and the municipal law of all countries except the US, the UK and the common law of Commonwealth states.

3.6.4   Case Indexes

There are a number of useful case indexes. These include:

- the Daily Law Reports Index which is issued fortnightly and is the most up-to-date index of the formal case reports from the 'quality' newspapers. It will include cases which were too late for publication in, for example, the latest Current Law Monthly Digest. It indexes under case name (alphabetical), subject-heading and legislation referred to. A quarterly cumulation gives full citations for cases cited in the major law reports.

- the Law Reports Index (the 'red books') indexes the Law Reports since 1951 in the form of one volume for each decade by case name and subject with alternative citations from other series of law reports

- the All England Law Reports Consolidated Index indexes cases reported in the All England Law Reports from 1936-92. Volume 1 indexes by case name, practice directions, statutes considered and words and phrases considered. Volumes 2 and 3 index by subject. It is up-dated by annual Tables and Indexes in the same format.

- the Weekly Law Reports Index
- the Legal Journals Index is issued monthly and includes a case name and subject index
- the English Reports Index (Vols 177 and 178) indexes in alphabetical order cases reported in the Nominate Reports before 1865. The reference to the location of the report in the English Reports is in bold type. In the absence of the name of the case, citations to the Nominate Reports can be cross-referenced using the Chart to the English Reports.

3.6.5   Indexes of Government Publications

- **Daily List of Government Publications (HMSO)**

  This contains a list of Parliamentary publications (House of Lords and House of Commons Papers and Bills, Command Papers, Acts and Debates), non-Parliamentary publications including statutory instruments and a list of publications of bodies such as the EC and the UN whose publications are sold, but not published, by HMSO.

- **HMSO Monthly Catalogue**

  This contains House of Lords and House of Commons Papers and Bills in number order, Command Papers in numerical order, a list of Acts published and a list of Parliamentary and non-Parliamentary publications (excluding Bills, Acts and debates) arranged by government department. There is also an **HMSO Annual Catalogue** and **Quinquennial Consolidated Index**.

3.6.6   Other General Indexes or Directories

You may have cause to consult the following:

- **The British Humanities Index**, which is published quarterly with annual cumulations, indexes newspaper articles and journals. It is especially useful in locating articles on the impact of law in society which are not to be found in the legal journals.

- **The Social Service Abstracts**. This monthly service, prepared by the Library Services of the Departments of Health and Social Security, includes references to and digests of legal articles relevant to the areas of social services and welfare.
- **Raistrick's Index to Legal Citations and Abbreviations.**

3.7   Quick find checklist

This checklist is not intended to be exhaustive. It suggests a number of quick alternative routes to finding information.

3.7.1   To find a case by name

- Use the Current Law Case Citators 1947-76, 1977-88, 1989-91
- Use the Law Reports Index or the All England Reports Consolidated Index

  If you cannot locate the case, it probably means it is either old (pre-1947 and not considered in a post-1947 case), very recent, or foreign.

- Use The Digest to trace older English or Scottish cases or cases from the Irish or Commonwealth courts
- Use the Case Citator in the most recent issue of the Current Law Monthly Digest or the case index to the Legal Journals Index to locate recent cases
- If the case is too recent for the Monthly Digest, consult the recent Weekly Law Reports Indexes and the Daily Law Reports Index

3.7.2   To trace the history of a case

- Use the Current Law Case Citator for the relevant period and all subsequent Citators to see if the case has been judicially considered
- Use the Case Citator in the latest issue of the Current Law Monthly Digest to up-date your information

3.7.3   To trace articles on a case

*   Use the Current Law Case Citators as above
*   Use the case index in the Legal Journals Index for articles from 1986
*   Use the case index in the Index to Legal Periodicals
*   Use the articles indexes in the Current Law Year Books 1976 and 1986 and in subsequent Year Books

3.7.4   To trace information by subject

*   Use the index of a relevant text
*   Use the Index to Halsbury's Laws and up-date using the Cumulative Supplement and the Current Service Monthly Review and Noter-Up

3.7.5   To trace cases by subject

*   Use the Law Reports Index or the All England Reports Consolidated Index
*   Use Halsbury's Laws as above
*   Use the subject indexes in the Current Law Year Books 1976 and 1986 and in subsequent Year Books. Then up-date by using the subject index of the latest Monthly Digest.
*   If the case is after 1985, use the subject index to the Legal Journals Index

3.7.6   To trace statutes by title

*   Use the Current Law Statute / Legislation Citator for the relevant period. Check for amendments or repeal using the subsequent Citators and the latest Monthly Digest.

3.7.7   To trace statutes by subject

*   Use the Consolidated Index to Halsbury's Statutes or, if recent, the index to the Cumulative Supplement. Up-date using the Cumulative Supplement and the Noter-Up.

3.7.8   To check whether legislation is in force

• Use Halsbury's Statutes as above

• Use the Current Law Legislation Citators and up-date using the Monthly Digest

• Use Is it in Force?

3.7.9   To trace statutory instruments by subject

• Use the Consolidated Index to Halsbury's Statutory Instruments and up-date using the Annual Cumulative Supplement and the Monthly Survey

3.8   Why to use What, and When

It would be unwise to be dogmatic in directing you to a particular reference volume for a particular purpose. The Current Law and Halsbury Series are, of course, competing services. Sometimes several equally effective methods are available. You will develop your own preferences. Some of the volumes are multi-purpose research tools. Not all of the reference works may be available in your library. Quite apart from this, the use of different resources may not yield identical results and it is always wise to check your findings via an alternative route. However, the following tips for quick information retrieval based on the author's preferences may be useful:

Use the Current Law Series

• for post-1946 research only

Use the Current Law Case Citator

• for alternative citations of cases decided after 1946

• as a quick reference for the post-1946 judicial history of any case decided at any time

• as a quick reference for articles on cases decided after 1946

• for references to digests of cases in the Current Law Year Book

Use the Current Law Legislation Citator

- as a quick reference for amendments and repeals made after 1946 to statutes of any date
- as a quick reference to cases decided on any legislative provision after 1946
- as a quick reference to statutory instruments issued after 1946

Use Current Law Statutes Annotated

- for the full *original* text of statutes with explanatory annotations
- for the derivation of consolidating statutes

Use the Current Law Monthly Digest

- for a comprehensive up-dating service
- to up-date the judicial history of cases from the latest issue of the Case Citator
- to up-date statutes from the latest issue of the Legislation Citator
- for summaries of recent cases
- for summaries of recent statutes
- for summaries of recent cases on quantum of damages
- for summaries of statutory instruments
- to identify whether a recent Bill has received the Royal Assent

Use the Current Law Year Book

- for summaries of cases in a particular year
- for summaries of Acts of a particular year
- for summaries of statutory instruments of a particular year
- for subject indexes of articles (or books) published in a particular year

Most of these objectives can be achieved using the Halsbury Series. In addition:

Use Halsbury's Laws

- to research a topic by subject

Use Halsbury's Statutes

- for the *amended* text of statutes with explanatory annotations

Use Halsbury's Statutory Instruments

- for the full text of statutory instruments

Use Halsbury's Digest (The English and Empire Digest)

- to find cases on a particular subject
- to locate references to pre-1947 cases

Use Halsbury's Is It In Force?

- as a quick guide to the commencement dates of statutes since 1967
- as a quick (but sometimes incomplete!) reference to statutory amendments or repeals since 1967

Use Statutes in Force

- for the text of current statutes as amended

Use the Index to the English Reports

- to find references to pre-1866 cases
- to find alternative citations in the English Reports for cases originally reported in nominate reports

Use the Legal Journals Index

- to locate articles written after 1985 by subject or author
- using the name of the plaintiff or defendant, to locate post-1985 articles which refer to particular cases

ALWAYS DOUBLE CHECK! NEVER CUT CORNERS!
ALWAYS UP-DATE!

Finally, let us now review how you might have found the
answers to the questions on the case of *Jeffrey v Black* posed at
the beginning of this chapter. It is not suggested that the following
are the only methods which could be used and you may have
found the same information via different routes.

1   Where would you find alternative citations for *Jeffrey v Black*?

Use the Current Law Case Citator 1977-88. You will find the
following alternative citations:

[1978] QB 490, [1977] 3 WLR 895, (1977) 121 SJ 662, [1978] 1
All ER 555, [1977] Crim LR 555.

2   How would you identify in which, if any, cases *Jeffrey v Black* has
    been (a) applied (b) distinguished (c) followed or (d) overruled?

Use the Current Law Case Citator 1977-88 and follow up the
references to the Current Law Year Book. You will find references
to 78/2568 and 85/665.

Jeffrey v Black has since been followed in *R v Warren (A) and
Warren (T)* [1985] Crim LR 252 (digested in the 1985 Year Book
at para 665) and applied in *R v Smith (Benjamin Walter)* [1978]
Crim LR 296 (digested in the 1978 Year Book at para 2568).

Up-date using:

* the Current Law Case Citator 1989-92
* the Cumulative Table of Cases in the latest Current
  Law Monthly Digest
* the Daily Law Reports Index.

Nil result.

Also, check the case report of *Jeffrey v Black* itself for stickers.
These will tell you that *Jeffrey v Black* was doubted in *R v Sang*
[1979] 2 All ER 46 and that a dictum of Lord Widgery CJ was
considered in *McLorie v Oxford* [1982] 3 All ER 480. This indicates

that using the Current Law Case Citator is a quick but not complete method of up-dating cases. It is always wise to check your research findings using an alternative method.

Another strategy is to use Archbold's Pleading, Evidence and Practice (see Chapter 4). Using the 1992 Tables and Index, you will find references to *Jeffrey v Black* in the Main Volumes at Chapter Fifteen paras 420 and 423 under the heading 'Evidence Obtained through Unlawful or Unfair Act or by Trickery'. This reviews the effect of the Police and Criminal Evidence Act ss 76(2)(b) and 78 and the cases of *R v Mason* (1988) 86 Cr App R 349, CA and *R v Jelen and Katz* (1990) 90 Cr App R 456 CA.

Also, using the cases index to Stone's Justices Manual (see Chapter 4), you will find a reference to *Jeffrey v Black* in volume 1 Chapter Two at para 120.

3   Where would you look for the full text of the provisions of the Police and Criminal Evidence Act which cover (i) legality of searches of premises and (ii) admissibility of evidence unlawfully obtained?

Use Current Law Statutes Annotated or Halsbury's Statutes.

Refer to Current Law Statutes Annotated for the relevant year (1984). The Police and Criminal Evidence Act is found in volume 4.

Each volume lists the statutes in chronological order by chapter number (the Act is c 60 for the Parliamentary session) and by short titles with references to the respective chapter numbers. The volumes are arranged in chapter order.

Look up the Act and use the Arrangement of Sections to identify the sections on (i) entry and search without a warrant (Part II ss 17 and 18) and (ii) exclusion of unfair evidence (Part VIII s 78).

Current Law Statutes Annotated may be checked for amendments/repeals using the Current Law Legislation Citator and the cumulative statute citator in the latest Monthly Digest.

Alternatively, if you know the sections you require, you may use Halsbury's Statutes. Using the Alphabetical List of Statutes in the Table of Statutes and General Index 1992-93, you will find references to ss 1-32 in Volume 12 at p 842 and to ss 68-82 in Volume 17 at p 207. If you are not sure which sections of the Act you require, you will need to formulate search terms and use the Subject Index. Using this method, the search term 'entry and search' will direct you to Volume 12 at p 863 where you will find s 18 and a note on *Jeffrey v Black*. The search term 'evidence, unfair, exclusion of' will direct you to Volume 17 at p 215 where you will find s 78 and a note on *R v Sang*.

4   Where would you locate cases decided on the relevant provisions of the Police and Criminal Evidence Act?

Use the Current Law Legislation Citator 1972-88. Look up the Act and proceed to the relevant provisions. For example, under s 18 you will find the case of *R v Badham* [1987] Crim LR 202 in Wood Green Crown Court. You will find numerous cases under s 78.

Up-date using:

- the Current Law Legislation Citator 1989-92
- the cumulative statute citator in the latest Current Law Monthly Digest

As at December 1992 you would find no references in either of these for s 18 but numerous references in both for s 78.

For example, in the Digest for April 1992 at para 79, you will find the case of *R v Kings Lynn Justices ex parte Holland* The Times April 6 1992 DC.

5   How would you find out whether the relevant provisions of the Police and Criminal Evidence are in force?

Use Is It In Force 1992? Statutes are arranged in chronological order and commencement dates are given for each provision. You will find that both ss 18 and 78 came into force on 1 January 1986.

To find out whether the provisions have been amended or repealed, you might use Halsbury's Statutes (which will also give you commencement dates), the Cumulative Supplement and Noter-Up. You will find that neither section has been amended or repealed to date.

6   How would you locate articles on *Jeffrey v Black*?

Use the Legal Journals Index to locate articles from 1986. Use the case index for each volume under 'Jeffrey' or 'Black' and the subject index for each volume (the indexes are not cumulative) using search terms such as 'police powers', 'Police and Criminal Evidence Act', 'search and seizure', 'admissibility'. You will find numerous references.

For example, several references are contained in the 1992 Volume 7 No 6 subject index at p 296 under 'search and seizure'. Further references are contained in the 1992 Vol 7 No 10 subject index at p 105 under 'Police' and 'Police Inquiries'. These refer you to *R v Horseferry Road Magistrates Court ex parte Bennett* The Times Sept 14 1992, *R v Christou* The Times June 1 1992 CA and to the 1992 Criminal Law Review at pp 729-733.

7   Where would you find a statement of the current legal position on each of these issues?

Use Halsbury's Laws. Locate references to the subject areas using the Consolidated Subject Index. Up-date using the Cumulative Supplement and Current Service. You may also use the Annual Abridgment.

Alternatively, use a specialist text - preferably one of the loose-leaf encyclopaedias - ensuring that your information is up-to-date.

3.9   End of chapter references and additional reading

Butterworths   *A User's Guide to Halsbury's Laws
                                      of England*

Butterworths   *A User's Guide to Halsbury's Statutes*

Butterworths   *A User's Guide to Halsbury's Statutory
                                      Instruments*

Butterworths   *A User's Guide to The Digest*

Clinch, P   *Using a Law Library*
(1992)   Blackstone Press

Dane, J and   *How to Use a Law Library*
Thomas, P   Sweet & Maxwell
(1987)

Sweet & Maxwell   *How to Use Current Law*

CHAPTER

4 The Practitioner's Law Library

4.1 From academia to practice

The previous chapter was concerned with the standard tools of the trade of the legal researcher - academic or practitioner - which you would expect to find in a medium-sized academic law library. It may be that nothing in that chapter was entirely new to you. However, there also exists a number of works with which it is likely you will have little, if any, familiarity. Even a university law library may not subscribe to some of them unless it offers a vocational course such as the Legal Practice Course. These are the standard works of the practitioner.

Practitioners' libraries vary enormously in quality. Indeed, you should not expect that the average solicitors' firm in the provinces will have its own library as such other than - perhaps - access to the Halsbury and/or Current Law series, a set of law reports, selected practitioner encyclopaedias and reference works (according to the nature of the firm's work) and some practitioner periodicals and journals. Even the larger City firms will not have comprehensive library facilities to compare with those which may have been available to you at your university. Even if they have the necessary financial resources to support a library, they may not have the necessary physical space. Of course, many of the journals considered to be necessary in an academic law library are of infrequent, if any, use to the practitioner.

If you are in the fortunate position of having alternative offers of traineeship, the library resources available may well influence your choice. However well equipped your firm's own internal library, you will certainly need access to other library resources at your local university, the Institute of Advanced Legal Studies if situated in the City, or the Law Society library. You will need to investigate the resources available both inside and outside the firm. If the firm has its own library, have a look at it. Does the firm subscribe to LEXIS? Does it have other databases? What other resources are available in the locality?

The material in this chapter is based on a review of the practitioner works which you are most likely to encounter whatever the nature or size of the practice. A sample of the more specialist works is also mentioned. In those firms where a true law library exists - largely the City firms (and then not all) - you will also find a law librarian, whose function will be essentially to maintain the most effective legal information system within the budget available to her/him and to assist partners and fee-earners (and perhaps trainees) in necessary research tasks. Some of the City and the larger provincial firms also have Directors of Legal Training, one of whose functions will be to provide trainees (and even partners!) with further instruction on research and other skills. Even if you are fortunate enough to have such personnel, your own research skills still need to be as fully developed as possible - the more so because firms with such resources are likely to engage in a range of specialisms. Your acquisition of research skills will never be complete. There is always more you can learn.

This chapter will provide a brief introduction to the standard practitioner works and how to to use them appropriately and effectively. In this chapter the practical exercises are not interspersed throughout the text but are contained at the end of the chapter, and require you to identify the appropriate research tool as well as demonstrate an ability to use it. Once you have completed the exercises, you can compare the method followed and results obtained with the sample answers provided.

The sample answers are based on use of the practitioner texts referred to in this chapter. Equal results can often be obtained by using the Halsbury or Current Law series. You are recommended to try both sources where appropriate and compare the results.

4.2   Encyclopaedias

The legal encyclopaedia is one of the main tools of the practitioner giving concise statements on the law and often containing the appropriate forms and precedents. A great many encyclopaedias are produced by the main law publishers, some of general interest whilst others are specialist in nature. Many are loose-leaf and so regularly up-dated (assuming efficient filing of the loose-leafs). The volumes which are of the most general interest are considered in some detail below along with a selection of the specialist volumes. You will soon become familiar with the encyclopaedias relevant to your specialist area(s) of expertise.

4.2.1   The Supreme Court Practice 1993 (The White Book) 10th ed Sweet & Maxwell

The Supreme Court Practice (commonly referred to as 'The White Book' because of its colour) contains the Rules of Court, reported cases on those Rules, and Practice Directions and Notes. It consists of two volumes plus a separate Index (by subject) and Tables of Cases, Statutes and Statutory Instruments. It is up-dated by cumulative supplements issued at six monthly intervals and the Supreme Court Practice News which is issued ten times a year. The publishers intend to publish a new edition every two years.

4.2.2   County Court Practice (The Green Book) Butterworths

The Green Book is regarded as a companion to the White Book and concentrates on County Court Rules and practice. It is produced annually with supplements as necessary.

4.2.3   Other specialist encyclopaedias

Specialist loose-leaf encyclopaedias include the Encyclopaedias of Banking Law, Consumer Credit Law, Data Protection, EC Law, Financial Services Law, Employment Law, Environmental Law and Practice, Housing Law and Practice, Insurance Law, Landlord and Tenant (Woodfall), Planning Law and Practice, Registered Conveyancing (Ruoff & Roper), Road Traffic Law and Practice, Town and Country Planning, and VAT. These are all published by Sweet & Maxwell. Clarke Hall and Morrison on Children, the Family Law Service, Garner's Environmental Law, Harvey on Industrial Relations and Employment Law, Hill and Redman's Landlord and

Tenant, the Personal Injury Litigation Service, Rayden and Jackson on Divorce, Tristram and Coote's Probate Practice and the Yellow and Orange Tax Handbooks are all published by Butterworths.

4.3   Precedents

As a practitioner, you will have numerous drafting tasks. These may involve the drafting of procedural documents such as writs, pleadings, interrogatories, affidavits or powers of attorney (if any of these terms needs explanation, use a law dictionary, below). They may involve drafting of documents which regulate parties' rights such as a contract, lease, conveyance, trust deed or will.

Needless to say, practitioners do not draft such documents afresh on each occasion they are needed. Exemplars have been developed over the years and compilations made in the form of precedent encyclopaedias. Firms also develop their own precedent documents. Of course, this does not mean that the student, trainee or practitioner will not have to adapt the precedent to meet particular circumstances and the client's particular objectives (see also 'Drafting' by Elmer Doonan in this series).

A general compilation of forms and precedents which you are likely to encounter at an early stage of your vocational training is the Encyclopaedia of Forms and Precedents.

4.3.1   The Encyclopaedia of Forms and Precedents (Butterworths)

This is a collection of the non-litigious forms and precedents necessary in practice. The 5th edition consists of 42 volumes with cumulative Noters-Up, Service Binders (5 volumes) and an annual Consolidated Index, currently up to 1 October 1992. Volumes after 1 October 1992 are covered by their own indexes. Coverage is comprehensive but may be scattered between the main volume and the service binder; for example, volume 9 on Companies contains precedents on memorandum and articles of association and Service Binder B includes precedents for off the shelf companies.

The Encyclopaedia is also useful as a quick and general reference tool since it does not simply contain precedents but also a review of the law, practice and procedure relevant to the precedent.

4.3.2   Atkin's Court Forms (Butterworths)

Atkins is a companion collection of forms and precedents to the Encyclopaedia of Forms and Precedents for the litigious areas of civil law. Consisting of 41 volumes, it is more comprehensive than the Green Book and includes court forms for all courts and tribunals in England and Wales (including the European Courts) with civil jurisdiction. Like The Encyclopaedia, it also provides a quick reference point for the law on the relevant subject area. The main volumes are up-dated by re-issue volumes, an annual supplement and an annual consolidated index. A volume re-issued after the index will contain its own index. Such volumes are marked with an asterisk in the Table of Current Titles in the latest Consolidated Index.

Halsbury's Laws is cross-referenced in each of these publications.

4.3.3

Specialist compilations of precedents include Longman's Commercial Conveyancing Precedents, Commercial Lease Precedents, Lending and Security Precedents, Will Precedents and Bullen and Leake's Precedents of Pleadings. Some of the practitioner journals also offer suggested precedents.

4.4   Other practitioner reference works

Archbold's Criminal Pleading, Evidence and Practice (Sweet & Maxwell) is the criminal lawyers' manual, consisting of two volumes and a separate volume of index (by cases, statutes, statutory instruments and subject) and tables. It provides a quick reference for points of criminal law, but is not loose-leaf nor supplemented, so you must ensure (as always) that you up-date.

Diagram III

Using The Encyclopaedia of Forms and Precedents

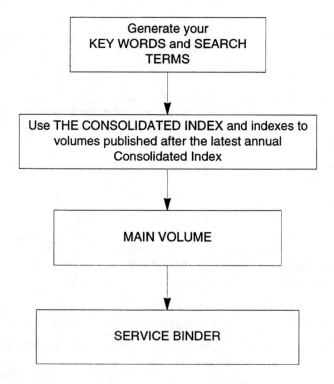

NB. The Encyclopaedia is accompanied by a Users' Guide

Stone's Justices Manual (Butterworths)

This is a reference work on criminal law and procedure, forms and precedents. It consists of three volumes with an index by statute/ treaty, case and subject at the back of volume 3.

Kemp & Kemp (Sweet & Maxwell)

Kemp & Kemp consists of three volumes on quantum of damages. It is an indispensible research tool for the civil litigator when dealing with personal injuries claims. In loose-leaf form, it is arranged according to the nature of the injury. In the case of claims involving multiple injuries, therefore, you need to refer to a combination of sections. Volume 1 also provides a review of the general principles of a personal injuries claim and the heads of damage (pecuniary and non-pecuniary, with pecuniary including pain and suffering, loss of amenities, loss of expectation of life, inconvenience, discomfort, disappointment and mental stress).

4.5   Professional conduct

As a practitioner you will also need to be able to access the standard works on professional conduct. It is essential that a solicitor conducts her/himself in a professional and ethical way as well as, of course, abiding by the general law. A failure to do so may result in an action for negligence or a hearing before the Law Society's Disciplinary Tribunal.

The Law Society publishes rules for its membership in its Guide to the Professional Conduct of Solicitors 1990 and the Professional Standards Bulletins. You will have been provided with a copy of the Society's Guide on registering as a Legal Practice Course student.

The Law Society's Written Standards for the Legal Practice Course require students to be familiar with the Rules of Professional Conduct which deal with the conduct of fee earning work of a type likely to be encountered before admission as a solicitor, in particular in relation to:

i)   the retainer

ii) fees - the standards on information as to costs and the basis of charging

iii) client care - Rule 15 of the Practice Rules

iv) handling clients' money - the need to keep office and client money separate and to pay interest to the client where appropriate

v)   conflicts of interests in contentious and non-contentious work, including particularly Rule 6 (the prohibition against acting for vendor and purchaser or lender and borrower in a private mortgage)

vi) confidentiality

vii) bad professional work and negligence

viii) the solicitor and the court

ix) professional undertakings

Students must also be aware but need not have a detailed knowledge of the Rules relating to the organisation of the profession (practising certificates and indemnity insurance, private practice, employed solicitors, legal advice centres, law centres and duty solicitor schemes, the Solicitors' Complaints Bureau, the Solicitors' Disciplinary Tribunal and the Compensation Fund), obtaining work (including the publicity codes), and professional relations with other solicitors, the Bar and non-lawyers. You will be required to become fully familiar with these Rules during your period of traineeship.

The Law Society has recently published Draft Practice Management Standards (see The Law Society Gazette 90/6 10 February 1993 at pp 33-36). These are intended to be 'a practical management tool which will benefit solicitors and their clients, if practices choose to make use of them'. It is worth noting that draft standard A3 requires practices to have procedures to ensure compliance with Practice Rule 15 (client care) and the professional standard on costs information 'and to provide for clear and regular communication with clients including the use of language that may be readily understood'.

Finally, Cordery on Solicitors provides guidance on solicitors' rights, privileges and disabilities, liabilities, negligence, remuneration, professional relationships, professional practice and conduct.

4.6   Specialist law reports

You will all be familiar with the Official Reports and the All England and Weekly Law Reports. You may well have had access to specialist series of law reports, in particular in the optional subjects you selected. There are a wide variety of specialist reports. These include the Building Law Reports, Construction Law Reports, Industrial Cases Reports, Employment Law Cases, Industrial Relations Law Reports, Housing Law Reports, Lloyd's Law Reports (Insurance), Fleet Street Reports, Reports of Patent Cases, Local Government Reports, Planning Law Reports, Property, Planning and Compensation Reports, Estates Gazette Reports, Rating and Valuation Reports, Road Traffic Reports, Reports of Tax Cases, and Simon's Tax Cases.

The advantage of the specialist reports is that their coverage is more extensive than the general series of law reports and they include, for example, the decisions of relevant tribunals.

4.7   Periodicals and journals

A wide range of periodicals and journals are issued at regular intervals, often weekly, and are a valuable source of practical and academic information and comment. You are likely to be familiar already with the New Law Journal. Those specifically aimed at the practitioner include the Law Society's Gazette, The Lawyer, the Solicitors' Journal, and The Practical Lawyer.

Some publications are hybrids of law reports and journals. They give synopses of cases with commentary on their effects and implications, with articles interspersed; see, for example, the IDS Brief (published by Income Data Services Ltd) on Employment Law and the Journal of Planning Law (Sweet & Maxwell).

4.8   Dictionaries

Law dictionaries include Mozley and Whiteley's Law Dictionary (Butterworths) and Black's Law Dictionary (West Publishing Co).

Stroud's Judicial Dictionary of Words and Phrases (Sweet & Maxwell) consists of 5 volumes plus a cumulative supplement. It provides references to cases where words or phrases have been interpreted and statutes where they are used.

Butterworth's Words and Phrases Legally Defined defines terms as used in Australia, Canada, New Zealand and the US as well as the UK with references to cases and statutes. It can, therefore, be used to gain a comparative common law perspective if needed.

An invaluable reference source for abbreviations is Raistrick's *Index to Legal Citations and Abbreviations* (Bowker Saur).

4.9   Directories

There are numerous publications which list the names and addresses and sometimes the specialisms of solicitors' firms and barristers' chambers. Some also provide background information on the larger City and provincial firms and provide a useful source for the traineeship seeker. These include The Law Society's Directory of Solicitors and Barristers and Shaw's Directory of Courts in the UK.

Butterworths Law Directory 1992 is an index to solicitors and barristers in private practice, commerce, local government and public authorities. It includes an international section for law firms with offices overseas and foreign law firms with branches in England and Wales. Butterworths International Law Directory indexes firms abroad by name and region.

Who's Who in the Law (ed Pritchard and published by Legalease) is 'a guide to eminent and well known figures in the day-to-day world of practising lawyers'.

The Legal 500: The Clients' Guide to UK Law Firms (John Pritchard) is a consumers' guide to the 500 largest law firms which identifies the firms' expertise. It is also a useful source for students seeking a larger firm for traineeship.

Chambers & Partners' Directory: A User's Guide to the Top 1000 Law Firms and all Barristers' Chambers includes lists of the 100 largest (in size) firms in London and smaller lists for the provinces with their specialisms. A useful Solicitors' A-Z reviews each firm's background, principal areas of work, recruitment and training. There is also an A-Z for the London Bar.

Hazell's Guide to the Judiciary and the Courts is an annual publication which gives a comprehensive list of HM judges and stipendiary magistrates, the addresses of tribunals and lists of chambers.

Butterworth's Legal Services Directory is a compendium of services for legal practitioners. Amongst the range of services included are bailiffs, process servers and debt-recovery agencies, arbitrators, expert witnesses and costs draftsmen.

4.10   Computer software packages

The opportunity for the use of computer technology by the legal practitioner is now considerable and expanding. It is perhaps also true to say, however, that the current generation of lawyers has not yet fully exploited the potential of rapid advances in technology.

Software packages now available range from simple word-processing (such as Word Perfect and Microsoft WORD 5.5) and spell or grammar checking (such as Grammatik) to document management (such as Folio Views) and research tools (such as LEXIS). There are also an increasing number of precedent packages available. EMail systems provide for internal communication by personal computer rather than written memo. Detailed instruction on the use of LEXIS and an introduction to JUSTIS are given in Chapter 5.

The range of services available is well demonstrated by the Financial Times online information service, FT PROFILE Business Information. This gives access to materials from over 200 international publications and information services. The user connects using a computer terminal and telephone line to find articles and reports on subjects (eg a particular industry or merger or acquisition) - or people - of interest. For example, a search on 'Richard Branson' will find all articles in which the subject is mentioned. This can be a useful public relations tool and is used by some City firms to research the nature of a client's or potential client's business and interests. However, at a current user rate of £1 per minute, it is an expensive commodity.

4.11   Practical exercises

Try answering the following questions using the practitioner works referred to in this chapter. These are not, of course, the only available sources. You may try the same questions using the works referred to in Chapter 3 and compare your products.

Exercise 1

What are the monetary limits on the jurisdiction of the High Court and County Court in Contract and Tort?

Exercise 2

A landlord seeks your advice on the circumstances in which it would be unlawful to evict a tenant and the penalty for an unlawful eviction.

Exercise 3

What aggravating factors will affect the length of sentence in the case of a conviction for rape?

Exercise 4

Find an explanation of the phrase 'donatio mortis causa'.

Exercise 5

What is meant by the terms 'ex rel' and 'ex parte'?

Exercise 6

Locate a specimen precedent for a request for a preliminary ruling from the High Court to the European Court of Justice.

Exercise 7

You have been instructed to draft a will. Your client wishes the will to provide, inter alia:

i)   that she is to be buried in the same grave as her mother. Your client lives in another parish;

ii) that her heart be available for transplant;

iii) that, since she suffers from a rare disease which causes her, on occasions, to appear lifeless, a direction be formulated to ensure that she is not buried alive.

Advise your client whether these objectives can be met and draft clauses accordingly.

Exercise 8

Find a form for making an applicaton to the European Commission on Human Rights.

Exercise 9

Your client has been a machine operator in a factory for the past 20 years. As a consequence of operating the machinery she has developed a repetitive strain injury commonly called 'golfers' elbow'. You are negotiating with her employers to reach a settlement. What figure would represent a fair settlement?

Exercise 10

Can (i) books and (ii) newspapers be sold on a Sunday under the Shops Act 1950?

4.12   Sample answers using practitioner works

Exercise 1

Use the White Book.

Generate key words or search terms appropriate for use of the Index and Tables volume, for example, 'jurisdiction' 'county court'. You will find 'jurisdiction' indexed as a main head with 'county court' listed below. This, in fact, refers you to 'county court' where used as a main heading and 'jurisdiction' is listed there as a sub-heading (an annoying but very common practice!). You will find as sub-sub headings 'contract' and 'tort', both of which refer you to 5533 (vol 2 at para 5533). There you will find Part II of the County Courts Act 1984 s 15(1) which you are told was amended by the High Court and County Court Jurisdiction Order SI 1991 No 724 Art 2(8) and Sched, Part I. This is not cross-referenced and so back to the Index of Statutory Instruments! There you will find a reference to para 5516 which informs you that the jurisdiction of the County Court and High Court is concurrent and refers you to a detailed commentary on the Courts and Legal Services Act in the 1990 Supplement to The Supreme Court Practice 1991. Para 5221 informs you that where the value of the action in Contract or Tort is less than £25,000, trial will be in the County Court unless the court, having regard to specified criteria, considers that it ought to be transferred to the High Court. Where the value is £50,000 or more, trial will be in the High Court unless commenced in the County Court and that court does not consider that it should be transferred.

Exercise 2

Use Archbold.

Identify key words and generate search terms eg 'eviction', 'tenant'. Use the Tables and Index volume. Searches under each of these terms refer you to chapter 29 paras 51-55. Locate these in volume 2 where you will find the relevant provisions of the Protection from Eviction Act 1977 s 1 (as amended) and the penalty on summary conviction under s 32(2) of the Magistrates Courts Act 1980 which is cross-referenced.

Exercise 3

Use Archbold.

Key word 'rape'. Index reference to chapter 20 paras 18-20. Aggravating factors are:

- violence over and above the force necessary
- the use or threat of use of a weapon
- that the rape was repeated or planned
- that the rapist has previous convictions
- that the victim was subjected to other indignities
- that the victim was very old or young
- that the effect on the victim was especially serious

The authority referred to is *R v Billam* (1986) 82 Cr App R 347.

A general fear of AIDS is not an aggravating factor according to *R v Malcolm* The Times November 28 1987, CA.

These authorities could quickly be followed up using the Current Law Case Citators 1977-88 and 1989-92 and the cumulative case citator in the latest Monthly Digest.

Exercise 4

Use Stroud.

An explanation with references to relevant case-law will be found in volume 2 at page 767. This information can then be up-dated by reference to the Cumulative Supplement at page 56 which refers you to *Sen v Henley* The Times March 6, 1991 and *Woodard v Woodard* The Times March 15, 1991. You would, of course, again need to up-date yourself beyond this point but Stroud can be used as a quick reference research tool if, for example, you could not immediately recall the name of a case on d.m.c. It should not normally be used as a stand-alone research tool.

Exercise 5

Use Black or another legal dictionary.

Exercise 6

Use Atkins Court Forms.

Find the search term 'European Court' in the Consolidated Index 1992. You will find the sub-heading 'preliminary ruling' and the sub sub-heading 'order for reference, High Court'. The reference is to volume 17 (1992 Issue) at page 327 where you will find the precedent.

Exercise 7

Use The Encyclopaedia of Forms and Precedents.

i) Using the Search term 'Burial', you will find references in the Consolidated Index to volume 6 at para 412 which deals with rights of burial and volume 6 at para 476 which provides a precedent for a direction as to the place of one's burial. There is no right to be buried outside one's own parish although it is possible with agreement.

ii) Using the search term 'Heart, donation for transplant' you will find references in the Consolidated Index to volume 6 paras 403 and 481. The former reviews the law contained in the Human Tissues Act 1961 and the formalities required. The latter provides a precedent for a direction by a donee for the use of her/his body for organ transplant.

iii) Using the search term 'Burial, alive, direction for prevention of', you will find references in the Consolidated Index to volume 6 at para 484. This provides you with a precedent.

Exercise 8

Use Atkins Court Forms.

In the Consolidated Index under 'European Commission on Human Rights, application to', you will find a reference to 17 235 [352]. Volume 17 at page 235 reviews the procedure for application to the Commission and page 352 et seq provides the form for application. Explanatory notes on completion of the form follow at pages 361-64.

Exercise 9

Use Kemp & Kemp.

Refer to volume 3, section on Upper Limbs, and in particular to section H8 on Repetitive Strain Injuries. The main decision referred to is that of *Ping v Esselte Letraset Ltd* [1992] PIDR 74, where the awards ranged from £3,000-8,000 plus future loss of earnings. Since the range is so wide, you will need further information to establish the severity of your client's injury.

Exercise 10

Use Stone's Justices Manual.

Using the subject index, you will find a reference under 'books' to 7-28381 and under 'newspapers' to 7-28398. Refer to the paragraphs in section 7. You will find that books can be sold from an airport terminal, main-line railway station or bus station as approved by the Secretary of State. Newspapers can be sold in any shop.

CHAPTER

5 Computer Information Retrieval Systems

'I see no reason to suppose that these machines will ever force themselves into general use'

The Duke of Wellington (1769-1852)
on steam locomotives

5.1 Computer database services

In recent years great strides have been made in the development and use of computer databases in law. These fall into two main groups. First, information retrieval systems have been developed which, when fed appropriate search terms by the user, will locate information stored in the computer's memory. Information retrieval systems are essentially law libraries stored on a computer system. The user can call up requested raw information at the push of a button. This information is then analysed and applied by the user. In contrast, the development of more sophisticated programmes known as 'expert systems' enable the computer to apply the information to a given set of facts and produce some sort of 'resolution', for example, possible answers to a legal problem. In the field of law, such expert systems are still in their infancy.

This chapter will introduce you to the major legal information retrieval systems available to the lawyer, in particular, LEXIS (a general database including UK, EC, international and foreign law) and JUSTIS CELEX (an exclusively EC database). The emphasis, however, will be on LEXIS as the most comprehensive system available.

You may have had the opportunity to use LEXIS and JUSTIS CELEX during your undergraduate studies although most institutions place restrictions on student access to LEXIS because of the expense. This is a consideration always to be remembered before having resort to LEXIS. In comparison, JUSTIS is a fixed database contained on CD-ROM. It does not, therefore, have an up-dating service equivalent to that of LEXIS but, once the capital necessary to purchase the CD-ROM has been invested, there are no user costs payable to the manufacturer.

This chapter will propose:

- that you experiment with generating key words and search terms appropriate for the effective use of computer information retrieval systems in law

- that you become familiar with the services offered by the respective systems

- that you consider how to make best use of such systems as legal research tools.

5.2   Introducing LEXIS

LEXIS is by far the largest and most comprehensive computer information retrieval service for lawyers available in the United Kingdom. It was launched on the United Kingdom market in May 1980 by Butterworth (Telepublishing) Ltd. LEXIS is, quite simply, a computerised law library. Instead of searching the library shelves, you search within libraries and files of information stored on a computer database. LEXIS holds within its memory much more than you will find in many, indeed most, law libraries in terms of UK, EC, Commonwealth, international and foreign materials. One particular advantage over the average law library is that it stores unreported cases in transcript form. Many of these cases will never be reported in the law reports and will never reach the library shelves.

You may already be aware of the potential use of LEXIS. You may already have had some hands-on experience. If so, this chapter will serve as a refresher on how to use LEXIS. If not, it will give you an introduction to the potential of LEXIS. The only way to appreciate the full potential of LEXIS and how to use that potential to best advantage is by active use and experimentation.

This chapter will involve you in active use of LEXIS and contains preliminary exercises to give you some idea of the ways in which LEXIS can be employed. Where the results of these exercises are given, the information is current up to 1 March 1993.

LEXIS is, however, an expensive commodity and you should receive some training before you are allowed unsupervised access to it. Training may be provided for you by your Director of Training or law librarian. Do not be tempted always to ask your librarian to undertake the research task for you. You will only realise the full potential of LEXIS and how it can be used creatively by personal use. Training is available at the BTL Training School. Useful addresses and contact numbers for training courses are given at the end of the text.

To use LEXIS you need a telephone line, a modem and a LEXIS terminal with keyboard and printer. LEXIS can now be used with certain approved personal computers enabling you to down-load the results of your research directly onto disk. Note that the instructions on how to use LEXIS in this chapter are based on use of a dedicated terminal. If you are using a PC, you can display a list of function keys using the Help facility (Alt and H).

As noted above, LEXIS is a computer assisted legal information retrieval service. It is **not** a legal research service which gives the answers to problems (an expert system).

'It is a service which, if used with legal knowledge, a grasp of the legal problem being researched, an understanding of primary and secondary source materials plus a lively imagination, can help the lawyer or accountant to retrieve from its vast libraries material which, when analysed, may prove to be precisely relevant or helpful in solving the problem being worked on.' (Butterworth Telepublishing, 'What is LEXIS'.)

LEXIS is a 'full text' service; that is, it contains everything which appears in the original documents (not indexed, edited or annotated). Every word contained in the original documents is indexed in the LEXIS computer files, with the exception of those words so commonly used that they are non-searchable, for example, 'if', 'as', 'and', 'or', 'his'. You will find a list of non-searchable words in Appendix I at the end of this chapter.

LEXIS includes a collection of English, Irish and Scottish legal materials. Over 3,000 new reported and unreported cases and over 1,000 statutes and statutory instruments are added each year. The collection of international legal materials includes libraries from the EC, the US, France and the Commonwealth. The English libraries include case-law from 1945 (tax cases from 1875), statutes and statutory instruments. The European libraries include European case-law from 1954 (the inception of the European Court of Justice).

5.3   How to use LEXIS

Before using LEXIS for the first time, familiarise yourself with the LEXIS keyboard (see Diagram I on page 99). You can try some hands-on experience by following the research exercises at the end of this section. Alternatively, you could use your own - previously planned - exercises based on a research problem on which you are currently working.

5.3.1   The LEXIS keyboard

The LEXIS keyboard is set out in traditional fashion. **Character keys** are located centrally with the space bar at the bottom. **Function keys** are located primarily to the top and to each side though some character keys double as function keys. Note, in particular, the following function keys:

FULL	- displays the full text of the document selected
KWIC	- displays your search words where located in the document selected with at least 25 words of text on either side
VAR KWIC	- displays your search words where located in the document with at least 50 words on either side. Alternatively, you can select the number of words to be displayed by keying in the number before pressing the function key.
CITE	- depending on which file you are in, displays a list of case citations, sections of statutes or statutory instruments. If you identify a case in CITE mode you want to explore, key in the number of the case and TRANSMIT. LEXIS will then display the case in KWIC mode. For a full display of the case, press FULL.
SEGMTS	- displays segments of documents (see 5.7 below)
NEXT PAGE	- displays the next page in the document being searched
PREV PAGE	- displays the previous page in the document being searched
ROLL UP/DOWN	- moves the page displayed up or down line by line

FIRST PAGE	- displays the first page of the document being searched
NEXT CASE	- displays the first page of the next document. If you want to move ahead more than one document, key in the number of documents you want to miss and press NEXT CASE.
PREV CASE	- displays the first page of the previous document. If you want to move back more than one document, key in the number of the documents you want to miss and press PREV CASE.
FIRST CASE	- displays the first page of the first document, ie the most recent document retrieved
DISP **DIF LEVEL**	- displays the documents retrieved at a different search level. First, key in the number of the level you want.
REQST (R) **TRANSMIT**	- displays a summary of your search requests
TIME (T) **TRANSMIT**	- displays how long you have been connected to LEXIS
PAGES (P) **TRANSMIT**	- displays the length in pages (22 lines) of the document being searched
HELP (H) **TRANSMIT**	- displays a series of help messages
CL'NT (C) **TRANSMIT**	- enables you to enter a new client code
MODFY (M) **TRANSMIT**	- enables you to modify your search term

You may wish to keep this list handy for easy reference once you begin to use LEXIS.

Diagram I
The LEXIS Keyboard

5.3.2   Signing on

By signing on, you will be taking the first step to access LEXIS
and are also telling LEXIS that you are an authorised user.
Butterworths will then know to which account the expenditure you
have incurred should be charged.

i)   make sure the power to the LEXIS terminal is on!

ii) access to LEXIS may vary according to equipment. You
     should find instructions on how to access LEXIS by your
     terminal. Follow these.

iii) once into LEXIS the screen will 'Welcome (you) to LEXIS'.

iv) type in your ID number (your firm may have an ID) and
     press TRANSMIT.

v)   you must name your search by typing in a reference (eg the
     name of your client) of up to 32 characters. This will assist you
     in future identification of the search for office purposes or if
     you wish to trace the search having down-loaded onto disk.
     LEXIS itself will store your named search only until the
     morning after you conducted it. Press TRANSMIT.

vi) LEXIS will now display a list of libraries in abbreviated form,
     as follows:

UK LIBRARIES

    ENGGEN - English General Library

    UKJNL   - United Kingdom Law Journals Library

    UKTAX - United Kingdom Tax Library

    ADMRTY - Admiralty Library

    SCOT   - Scots Law Library

    NILAW   - Northern Ireland Law Library

REPUBLIC OF IRELAND LIBRARY

    ITELIS   - Republic of Ireland Law Library

COMMONWEALTH LIBRARIES

COMCAS - Commonwealth Law Library

AUST - Australian Law Library

NZ - New Zealand Law Library

CANADA - Canadian Law Library

EC LIBRARY

EURCOM - European Communities Law Library

INTERNATIONAL LIBRARY

INTLAW - International Law Library

FRENCH LIBRARIES (in French)

INTNAT - International Library including the Official Journal of the EC

LOIREG - Law and Regulations Library

PRESSE - French Press Agency and Le Monde

PRIVE - Private Cases Library

PUBLIC - Public Cases Library

REVUES - Reviews

Key in the library to which you want access. For example, for UK national law and EC law, you will need to access the ENGGEN and EURCOM libraries respectively. Only one library can be accessed at any one time. Press TRANSMIT.

vii) LEXIS will now display the files in the library selected. For example, the ENGGEN library includes files of cases, statutes, statutory instruments and tax materials. Key in the file you want. Press TRANSMIT.

LEXIS consists of a number of LIBRARIES. Each library contains a number of FILES and each file contains a number of DOCUMENTS.

You should now have successfully entered LEXIS. If so, the cursor will appear in the top left-hand corner of your screen. Those of you who use computers will be familiar with the cursor. As you type, the cursor will move one space to the right of the last character typed.

You are now ready to commence your search.

5.4   Key words and search terms

LEXIS does not have a brain; it has a **memory**. It will search the whole of the file you have accessed for the precise word(s) or phrase(s) you feed into its memory. So, for example, if you access the ENGGEN library and, within that library, the CASES file, LEXIS will search all the text of all the cases (DOCUMENTS) in the file to identify for you those in which your search term has been used.

You should plan your research in advance and have generated appropriate search terms before accessing LEXIS (see also Chapter 2). You need to be neither too general nor too specific in the formulation of your search term. A search using, for example, the term 'negligence' would be too general. It would locate many hundreds of cases where the word has appeared, most of which would not be relevant to your research task or, if relevant, easily accessible through alternative and inexpensive means. LEXIS will quickly tell you if your search term would retrieve more than 1000 documents. You are not charged for such a search and can re-formulate your search term, ie you can try a new search term. You cannot, however, simply modify your existing search term by adding other words (see below); you will have to start again. Remember also that some words are so common that LEXIS is programmed not to search for them (see Appendix 1 at the end of this chapter).

On the other hand, too specific a search term will yield too limited a response and may exclude relevant information. You will develop the skill of selecting search terms from reasoned preparation and with practice. You are best advised to commence a search with a sensibly restricted search term and then to subsequently refine your search by **modifying** your search term (see below). If your search term locates what appears to be an excessive number of cases (but less than 1000), you will need to modify your search by narrowing your search term. Alternatively, if your search term locates only one or two cases, you may need to broaden it. LEXIS allows you to narrow or broaden your request, using the **modify** procedure outlined below.

LEXIS will store each stage of your research in **levels**. Your initial research will be stored at Level 1. Once you have completed a level 1 search as above, you can proceed to **modify** it. LEXIS will then store an initial modification at Level 2, a second modification at Level 3 and so on. You can then move around within these levels.

In order to **modify** your search term to restrict the search:

1 Press MODFY.

2 Press TRANSMIT.

3 Key in your **connector** (see para 5.5 below) and your additional search word(s) (for example, 'negligence and shock').

4 Press TRANSMIT.

LEXIS will now conduct a search at Level 2.

You may, however, find that your search at Level 1 was already too restricted and wish to broaden it.

In order to **modify** your search at Level 1 so as to extend the search:

1 Press MODFY.

2 Press TRANSMIT.

3 Starting with a **connector**, key in further search terms (for example, 'negligence or nuisance') or alter existing terms using the cursor and editing keys.

4 Press TRANSMIT.

You may modify to restrict or broaden your search within any level. If you have conducted a search at several levels, select the level you want to modify by keying in the number of the level after pressing the MODFY key at stage 1 above. Always use the modify facility in preference to starting a new search. Each search attracts a fee but to modify is free.

As an alternative to modifying your search, which will change the form of the search being undertaken, you can now also request LEXIS to search within the documents already retrieved by using the FOCUS feature. So, for example, if you had undertaken a search relating to child trespassers (the search term 'child! w/5 trespass!' - asking LEXIS to retrieve cases where the word 'child' appears within five words of the word 'trespass' - identified 73 cases at 1/3/93) and wanted to identify which of the documents retrieved referred to railways, simply key in 'FOCUS' and press 'TRANSMIT'. LEXIS will then ask you to transmit your FOCUS search request. Key in 'rail!' and press 'TRANSMIT'. LEXIS will search the text of the documents you have already retrieved and tell you how many include the words 'rail', 'railway(s)' etc (35 cases). When you want to return to your original search, simply key in 'EXIT' and press 'TRANSMIT'.

5.5   Connectors

You may link words, phrases or numbers by using special commands known as **connectors**. The connectors you might find the most useful are 'and', 'or' and 'w/'. In this way you can make your search more specific and increasingly sophisticated or more general. Look at the following examples using the ENGGEN library and Cases file:

1   Using the search term 'nuisance and cricket', LEXIS will locate each case in which the words 'nuisance' and 'cricket' have appeared anywhere in the text (31 cases as at 1/3/93). LEXIS will not (cannot) search for the word 'and'. It will identify the word as a **connector**.

2   Using the search term 'nuisance and cricket or nuisance and football', LEXIS will locate each case in which the words 'nuisance' and 'cricket' have appeared anywhere in the text and also those cases in which the words 'nuisance' and 'football' have appeared somewhere in the text (45 cases). You could, of course, have made these the subject of two different searches, but you would have cost your firm two search fees. Note the formulation of the above search carefully. What words or phrases would the search term 'nuisance and cricket or football' have located? (63 cases).

3   Using the search term 'cricket w/15 football', LEXIS will locate each case in which the word 'cricket' appears within 15 words (the reference to '15') of 'football'. This is a useful search method when identifying cases with shared characteristics. For example, the search term 'football or cricket w/20 fire' will locate all those cases in which the words 'football' or 'cricket' have appeared within 20 words of 'fire'.

This strategy can also be useful for locating references to particular cases or statutes. For example, you may know of the case of *Miller v Jackson* and wish to up-date using LEXIS. If the case is only ever cited as *Miller v Jackson* then that may be your search term. LEXIS does recognise the 'v' as a search term. But the full citation of the case might be (in fact, it is not) *Miller and Watts v Jackson & Partners*. Either citation, or a variation, may have been used by the judges in referring to the case. By using the search term 'Miller w/5 Jackson', LEXIS will locate citations for the case of *Miller and Watts v Jackson & Partners* (had it existed) and all cases in which it had been cited. Some cases are also commonly referred to in abbreviated form, for example, the *Wednesbury case* (*Associated Provincial Picture Houses v Wednesbury Corporation*) and the full case name may not be an appropriate search term.

Exercise caution here. Do not automatically use the names of the plaintiff and/or defendant to locate a case. Remember that LEXIS conducts a literal search and will identify all documents which contain your search term. A case name may be common, eg *R v Smith*. Alternatively, the same case may have been cited in a number of contexts (for example, in relation to the legality of searches and admissibility of evidence unlawfully obtained) and you may be interested to identify only where a case has been cited in a particular context. If so, you might key in the less common name using a connector and a search term which identifies what the case is about or its context. For example, the search term 'Jeffrey w/25 search' should locate the case of *Jeffrey v Black* itself and those cases in which it has been cited in the context of 'search' (2 cases are identified whereas the search term 'Jeffrey v Black' itself identifies 13 cases).

Similarly, a connector may be useful when locating a reference to a statute in cases. Statutes may be variously described by judges and it may be unwise to use the short title of the Act. On the other hand, the substance of the Act may be general in nature and you would have to refine your search term. Imagine, for example, that you wished to retrieve cases which referred to the Occupiers Liability Act 1984. The search term 'occupiers liability' is too broad (370 cases) unless you wanted to review the entire development of the law relating to occupiers liability since 1945! The search term 'Occupiers Liability Act 1984' may prove too specific (4 cases). The search term 'Occupiers Liability w/5 1984' retrieves 6 cases because, for example, cases using the phrase 'Occupiers Liability Acts 1957 and 1984' were also retrieved.

Take another example. How would you formulate a search term to locate cases which refer to the Police and Criminal Evidence Act 1984? You might extract the key words 'Police and Evidence'. This search term would, of course, be far too broad. LEXIS would identify 'and' as a connector and retrieve all documents in which both words appeared anywhere in the text. LEXIS indicates that over 1000 cases are likely to be retrieved. Using the short title 'Police and Criminal Evidence Act 1984' retrieves 408 cases whereas 'Police and Evidence w/5 1984' retrieves 524.

We need to refine our search term. It may be that we are interested in a particular section of the Act. Using the search term 'Police and Evidence w/5 1984 w/10 78' is likely to retrieve all cases which refer to section 78. This search term retrieves 139 cases. Still too many? If so, we may refine our search by reference to date. The search term 'Police and Evidence w/5 1984 w/10 78 and date aft 1991' retrieves 24 cases. (Always remember to use the connector 'and' before 'date aft'.)

Remember also when searching for statutory provisions not to use the word 'section'. It is too common and may also be referred to in a number of ways, for example, 's', 'ss' or 'sect'. You could use the connector 'or' to connect each of these but this would not be worthwhile - simply use the section number alone as in the above example.

5.6   Alternate spellings

You will realise by now that accurate spelling of your search term is essential. LEXIS can only operate on the data which you feed into it. If that data is literally incorrect, LEXIS will search for the incorrect version. It may find something, but not what you are looking for. Always check your search term carefully once you have entered it and before you transmit. However, sometimes the spelling of words may vary and alternative spellings may appear in the data you want LEXIS to search. A number of techniques have been programmed into LEXIS to assist you.

5.6.1

An asterisk can be keyed into a word in place of a letter. LEXIS will then search for the search term with any letter where you have placed the asterisk. For example, using the search term 'beg*n', LEXIS will locate the words 'begun', 'begin', 'began'. An asterisk will, however, represent one character only. So, for example, the search term 'ste*ens*n' will locate the words 'stevenson' and 'stevensen' within the text being searched, but not 'stephenson'.

5.6.2

An exclamation mark keyed in (SHIFT & !) at the end of a word will locate that word with any suffix within the text being searched. For example, the search term 'negligen!' will locate the words 'negligent', 'negligently' and 'negligence'. Here, the exclamation mark replaces any one or number of characters needed to complete words. However, you need to exercise some caution here to ensure that your search term will limit the search to the words you actually want. So, for example, by use of the search word 'child!', LEXIS will search for 'child' and 'children' but will also search for 'childless', 'childlike', 'childish' and 'childishly'.

5.7   Using segments

Each document stored on LEXIS is sub-divided into a number of parts (segments), each of which can be searched separately. A case, for example, is sub-divided into the name of the case, the court in which the case was heard, the formal citation, hearing dates, judgment date, catchwords preceding the headnote, the headnote itself, introduction, the names of counsel, panel of judges, individual judges, judgments, the order made and names of solicitors.

You can use this facility by asking LEXIS to search for your search terms within a particular segment rather than searching the whole of the document. For example:

- if you wish to locate a case but know only part of the name, key in 'name' followed by your search word(s) in brackets and press TRANSMIT. LEXIS will search the name segment only of each of the files stored in its memory and locate those cases in which your search words appear in the title. For example, the search term 'name (Jeffrey)' currently identifies 33 cases and 'name (Black)' 73 cases.

- if you wish to locate a case(s) decided on a particular date, in a particular year, or before or after a particular date/year, key in your search terms followed by 'and date is' or 'and date aft' or 'and date bef' followed by the relevant date or year as appropriate. For example, 'Jeffrey v Black and date aft 1980' currently identifies 5 cases. This is especially useful for up-dating your knowledge.

- similarly, you can ask LEXIS to locate all cases in which a particular judge has given judgment by keying in 'writtenby' followed by the name of the judge in brackets eg 'writtenby (Scarman)'. This search term currently identifies 485 cases whereas 'writtenby Scarman LJ' identifies 165 cases.

Should you wish, LEXIS can also locate all cases in which a particular counsel has appeared. Simply key in 'counsel' followed by the name sought in brackets. Likewise, you can search for the names of cases in which a particular firm of solicitors has been involved.

5.8 Statutes

You will find statutory materials on the files in LEXIS named STAT, SI and STATIS. The STAT file contains all public general statutes of England and Wales, as amended. The SI file contains statutory instruments published under the Acts in the STAT file. The STATIS file combines the above materials.

In these files, each section of an Act or schedule (or part thereof) is stored as a separate document called an 'Item'. Similarly with each individual rule, regulation or article of a statutory instrument.

As with cases, both statutes and statutory instruments are divided into the following **segments** (as below) to enable you to locate words where they appear in a particular segment rather than LEXIS searching the entire document:

- title
- date
- authority
- cross-heading
- section
- date in force
- text
- annotations

Using the title segment, LEXIS will locate all sections in force of the document; using the section segment, LEXIS will locate a particular section; using the annotation segment, LEXIS will locate all sections of previous legislation which have been amended by the document identified; using the authority segment, LEXIS will locate all statutory instruments made under the statute identified. As with cases, simply key in the segment name followed by your search word(s) in brackets.

5.9   Typing and editing

When you type in your selected search words separate each word, and any connector, with the space bar. You do not need to use capital letters at all. Ensure that your search words are spelt correctly - LEXIS can only find words entered into the database and will not correct mistakes by the user! If you enter a term incorrectly, for example by misspelling a word, or wish to change the entry, then you may EDIT by re-locating the cursor to the point of revision using one of the direction keys located around the home key to the bottom right of the keyboard. You may then delete characters simply by typing over them, insert characters by pressing the INSERT key (press the key again to cancel the instruction once the insertion is complete) or delete a character located above the cursor by pressing the DELETE key (press again to cancel the instruction). Characters to the right of the cursor may be deleted by using the space bar. Once you have completed your search term, make sure the cursor is located at the end of the term and press the TRANSMIT key. LEXIS will now commence the search.

5.10   Viewing

Once LEXIS has completed your search at any level, you can view the results using the function keys as noted above in para 5.3.1.

5.11   Printing

Press PRINT and the text on the screen will be printed on the printer attached to the terminal (no charge). If you want to print more of the document, press NEXT PAGE and PRINT. Each printed page on LEXIS is only 22 lines. If you want to print from screen, check the length of the document using PAGES (SHIFT P) and TRANSMIT. To print a long document from screen will incur considerable on-line charges.

Press PRINT CASE and the full document will be printed at BTL and sent to you (charge).

Press MAIL IT and FULL and the full text of all your research at your last search level will be printed at BTL and sent to you (charge).

Press MAIL IT and CITE and the citations of cases or sections at your last search level will be printed at BTL and sent to you (charge).

Press MAIL IT and SEGMTS and the segments of the documents at your last search level will be printed at BTL and sent to you (charge).

Press MAIL IT and KWIC and the sections of text at your last level containing your search words will be printed at BTL and sent to you (charge).

Remember, if you are accessing LEXIS from a PC and not a dedicated terminal, you can down-load onto a disk and print your findings from the disk in the normal way.

5.12   Signing off

On completion of your search, you must remember to sign off.
Never forget to do this as otherwise charges will continue to be
incurred. Using the LEXIS terminal, proceed as follows:

1 Press the SIGN OFF key.

2 If you wish to store your research for later completion, press
   Y and then TRANSMIT. Your research will be saved - but
   only until the next morning!

3 If you have completed the research and do not wish to store
   your work so far, press N and TRANSMIT.

   LEXIS now disconnects.

   Remember, you will need to formulate what you think will be an
effective search term **before** you access LEXIS, otherwise you will
be incurring unnecessary expenditure. Once you are on-line,
charges will be made for the telephone connection and for each
search made. (Each search of a small, medium, large or very large
file costs £14.50, £15.50, £16.50 and £17.50 respectively. Connect
time is £21 per hour. Mail-Its and Print Documents cost 4p per line.
Screen prints, modify and focus facilities are free of charge.
(These costs are current at 1/3/93.) In planning your research and
identifying an appropriate research methodology, you need to be
cost effective. LEXIS may be a very efficient research tool but it is
expensive and should not be used when you have easy alternative
access to the materials you are seeking. The materials may be
available free of charge in your firm's library or your local university
library or, if not needed immediately, through inter-library loan.

5.13   LEXIS exercises

To help you to understand how LEXIS works, look at the following
exercises and follow one or more of them through at the LEXIS
terminal. Once you are sufficiently confident, formulate LEXIS
search terms for a research problem you are currently working on
and implement this part of your research plan at the LEXIS terminal.

Read each exercise carefully before you go into LEXIS.

Exercise 1: Discovery tour of LEXIS functions

1 Follow stages 1-5 under Signing On at para 5.3.2 above.

2 Go into the ENGGEN library (Type ENGGEN and press TRANSMIT).

3 Go into the CASES file (Type CASES and press TRANSMIT).

4 Type SALE W/2 GOODS AND MERCHANTAB! AND DATE AFT 1988. (This need not be typed in capital letters.) Press TRANSMIT.

   This search term makes use of the connectors 'w/2' and 'and', the suffix-searcher '!' and the date locator 'and date aft 1988'. LEXIS will search for individual cases (documents) within the CASES file which (i) contain the word 'sale' within 2 words of 'goods' and (ii) contain words beginning with 'merchantab' and (iii) are dated after 1988.

5 Once LEXIS has completed the search, it will tell you how many cases it has located with your search term. This will be a Level 1 search (15 cases retrieved as of 1/3/93).

6 Press CITE and LEXIS will display the names of the cases found.

7 Press PRINT and your printer will print the text on screen. If the case list is not complete, press NEXT PAGE followed by PRINT.

8 Press 1 and TRANSMIT. LEXIS will display a brief statement about the first case on the list.

9 Use the FULL, CITE, KWIC, VAR KWIC, SEGMTS, PAGE and CASE keys to discover the different ways in which LEXIS can manipulate this information.

10 Sign off if you are not proceeding to Exercise 2. Press the SIGN OFF key and follow the instructions on screen. You do not wish to store your research.

Exercise 2: Retrieving cases

Your client, Mrs Gray, seeks your advice.

> Mrs Gray owned the freehold of a large house which became too expensive for her to maintain. She therefore sold the freehold to Mr White who agreed to lease part of the house to her. The terms agreed were that for the first 5 years the rent payable was to be £1,000 pa. Thereafter, no rent would be payable until Mr White had converted the house into flats. Mrs Gray was to have her choice of flat at a reasonable rent.

> After 7 years, Mr White died. He left the freehold of the house to his son. The son wants vacant possession so that he can demolish the house and build an office block. He claims that Mrs Gray is a mere licensee and not a lessee protected by the Rent Acts.

This fact situation raises the distinction between leases and licences and is further complicated by the fact that Mrs Gray's occupation is currently rent-free.

Before reading further, formulate possible search terms.

1   Follow the steps for Signing On to LEXIS.

2   You want the English law library and so type ENGGEN. Press TRANSMIT.

3   You want the cases file and so type CASES. Press TRANSMIT.

4   You should have formulated your search terms before entering LEXIS.

   A search term such as 'LEASE AND LICENCE' will not be efficient. LEXIS would search for all cases which contain both of those words anywhere in the text. It would recognise 'AND' as a connector. It is likely that LEXIS would identify many cases not relevant to your needs.

   As you want to clarify the distinction between a lease and a licence, a more restricted and effective search term might be 'LEASE! OR TENAN! W/5 LICEN*E W/10 DISTIN!'.

   Using this search term, LEXIS will search for cases with the words 'lease', 'leases' (LEXIS automatically searches for both singular and plural), 'leasehold(s)', 'tenant(s)', 'tenancy(ies)' within 5 words of 'licence', itself within 10 words of 'distinction(s)' or 'distinguish(es)(ing)'. You may not be sure how to spell licence or may anticipate misspellings in the text. Hence use of the * (69 cases retrieved).

5   You may wish to inspect the cases retrieved using the CITE, KWIC and FULL keys.

6   Alternatively, you may wish to narrow your search by reference to the fact that occupation was rent-free. Press MODFY to modify your search and use a connector to refine your search term as follows: 'AND RENT W/2 FREE OR NO'.

This term requires LEXIS to search for the additional word 'rent' within 2 words of 'free' (so including not only 'rent-free' but 'free of rent') or 'no rent'.

This search will be at Level 2 (23 cases retrieved).

7   Press CITE to list the cases retrieved and use KWIC and FULL to view extracts.

8   Move from case to case using NEXT CASE, PREVIOUS CASE, FIRST CASE.

9   Sign off if you are not proceeding to Exercise 3.

Exercise 3: Retrieving statutes

You wish to locate relevant statutory provisions in the field of Intellectual Property Law dealing with devices to overcome copy protection. Formulate a search term.

1   Follow the steps for Signing On to LEXIS.

2   You want the English law library and so type ENGGEN. Press TRANSMIT.

3   You want the statutes file and so type STAT. Press TRANSMIT. If you were already in the ENGGEN library CASES file for Exercise 2, you could simply change files by pressing CHG FILE and then STAT and TRANSMIT. To enter a new search, press NEW SEARCH.

4   You will be searching for a provision of the Copyright, Designs
    and Patents Act. You cannot use the title of the Act itself as
    this would retrieve the Act in its entirety.

5   As each section, schedule and so on of a statute is a
    separate document in LEXIS, typing in a search term such
    as 'DEVICE AND COPY PROTECTION', will retrieve each
    section, schedule or other item which includes the words
    'device' and 'copy protection'. You have, therefore, narrowed
    your search to your needs. (2 items retrieved - the preamble
    to the Act and section 296 with full text if needed and the
    commencement order.)

6   Sign off if you are not proceeding to Exercise 4.

Exercise 4: Retrieving statutory instruments using segments

The Data Protection Act 1984 enables the Secretary of State to
establish a fee for registration under the Act. What is the current
fee? Formulate a search term.

1   Follow the steps for Signing On to LEXIS.

2   You want the English law library so type ENGGEN. Press
    TRANSMIT.

3   You want the statutory instruments file and so type SI.
    (Alternatively, you might use the STATIS file.) Press TRANSMIT.

4   Type in your search term, for example, 'AUTHORITY (DATA
    PROTECTION)'. As there is only one Data Protection Act, you
    do not need to include the year in your search term. You are
    searching using the authority segment and so LEXIS will
    search for statutory instruments made under the authorising
    statute identified - the Data Protection Act. This search term
    will retrieve all statutory instruments made under the Act and
    may, therefore, be too wide for your needs (66 items retrieved).

5   Modify your search term in order to narrow it. Press MODFY
    and TRANSMIT. Type in a connector to narrow your search
    as follows: 'AND FEE'. This second level search will search all

the documents retrieved and identify those in which the word 'fee' appears (11 items retrieved including the Data Protection (Fees) Regulations, in force 1 June 1991 and the Data Protection Registration Fee Order SI 1991 No 1142. This provides for a registration fee of £75).

6 Use the KWIC and FULL keys to locate the relevant document.

7 Sign off.

5.14 LEXIS library contents

Below is a brief review of some of the libraries and files held on LEXIS as at March 1993. It is by no means exhaustive. In particular, the very extensive US libraries are omitted. To obtain a complete list of LEXIS holdings, you will need to access the LEXIS library list and then go into each of the libraries to examine the list of files held. Alternatively, you can obtain the library contents and price list from Butterworths.

The English General Library - ENGGEN

Contains a file on cases (CASES), statutes (STAT), statutory instruments (SI), a combined file of statutes and statutory instruments (STATIS), tax files (DTAX and TAXMAT) and files for practising LEXIS search techniques (LEARN and LRNSTA).

The CASES file contains cases reported since January 1945 in some 48 series of general and specialist law reports and transcripts of unreported cases since 1980.

UK Law Journals Library - UKJNL

Contains files on articles published in the Estates Gazette (EG), the Law Society Gazette (LSG), the New Law Journal (NLJ), the Journal of the Law Society of Scotland (JLSS) and a combined file covering all of the above (ALLJNL).

Special topic and national and international law libraries include

UK Tax Library: UKTAX

Admiralty Library: ADMRTY

Scots Law: SCOT

The Law of Northern Ireland: NILAW

Irish Law: ITELIS

UK, Australian, New Zealand, Scots, Irish and Northern Ireland Law: COMCAS

Australian Law: AUST

New Zealand Law: NZ

European Community Law: EURCOM. The Cases file includes decisions of the European Court of Human Rights.

International Law: INTLAW. The EC Law file includes abstracts from the Official Journal of the EC in English.

French Law: INTNAT, LOIREG, PRIVE, PUBLIC and REVUES. The Intnat library contains the full text of the Official Journal of the EC in French.

5.15   A LEXIS checklist

1   Do you need to use LEXIS? Is the information you want easily available elsewhere?

2   Do you know what you want LEXIS to find?

3   Which library do you wish to search? Which file within the library?

4   Have you prepared your search term?

5   Is your search term likely to achieve your desired outcome? Is it too broad or narrow?

6   If your search term proves to be too broad/narrow, will you be able to modify it? Have you prepared alternative modifiers?

7   Have you considered fully how LEXIS will interpret your search term?

8   Does any word have an alternative spelling? If so, have you used * as appropriate?

9   Might there be alternative words to the ones you have used (for example, lessee/tenant)? If so, have you used the connector 'or'?

10 Might one of your key words have different suffixes (for example, trespass/trespasser/trespassing)? If so, have you used '!'?

11 Do you want LEXIS to search the whole of each item in a file? If not, have you selected the appropriate SEGMENT?

Remember

- be thoroughly prepared
- try to use LEXIS quickly and efficiently
- use the MODIFY or FOCUS facilities in preference to starting a new search
- store your findings if you intend to resume your search
- always remember to SIGN OFF

5.16   JUSTIS

JUSTIS is a package produced by Context Ltd designed to operate a series of databases either on-line or held on CD-ROM using an IBM compatible personal computer. Once JUSTIS is installed in the PC's hard disk it will operate in conjunction with the CD-ROM in the CD-ROM drive. Databases held on CD-ROM include JUSTIS WL-CD (the Weekly Law Reports January 1985 - date), SI-CD (Statutory Instruments January 1987 - date), JUSTIS SM CD (the Single Market database), SCAD+CD (the official bibliographic database of the European Communities), JUSTIS CELEX and JUSTIS OJC (see below). Some of the CD-ROMS (for example, CELEX) have more than one database which can be searched individually or in combination. The Times and The Independent law reports are also available on-line.

CELEX is the official legal database of the European Communities and covers primary legislation (the treaties), secondary legislation (regulations, directives and decisions), preparatory works including summaries of future legislation and proposals from the Commission to the Council of Ministers, all case-law of the European Court of Justice since 1961, national law which implements EC law and, finally, European Parliamentary questions.

JUSTIS OJC was launched in November 1992 as a companion to CELEX. It contains the full text of the C Series of the Official Journal of the European Communities which includes proposed legislation, notices of European Court of Justice cases and activities of the European Parliament. The first disk covers the period January 1990-June 1992.

The principles which regulate the use of JUSTIS are not dissimilar from those which you have used to operate LEXIS. The detailed JUSTIS User Manual is itself contained on CD-ROM with an accompanying tutorial. As with LEXIS, you need to construct a 'query' using search terms and 'logical operators', such as 'and', 'or' or 'not' to connect your search terms.

The advantage of using JUSTIS is that, once the CD-ROMS have been purchased, there are no on-line charges and you can afford to be more leisurely in conducting a search. The disadvantage is that JUSTIS is not immediately up-to-date. JUSTIS CELEX and Single Market are up-dated every 3 months although a JUSTIS On-Line Service is up-dated each week and CD-ROM users can register as 'pay as you go' On-Line users. JUSTIS WL-CD, SI-CD and SCAD+CD are up-dated every 6 months. Each new disk issue up-dates and replaces the previous disk.

Research findings can be down-loaded onto disk for storage and printing. Training courses are available and these often carry Law Society Continuing Education points.

5.17   LAWTEL

LAWTEL is one of the databases which can be accessed on the British Telecom Prestel service. It contains a digest of current law including Bills, Acts, statutory instruments, Green and White papers. To operate LAWTEL you do not formulate search requests. LAWTEL is indexed and you simply follow the menu paths displayed along the route to the information you wish to access. The system includes a tutorial to assist you in learning how to operate it. It is up-dated daily but does not include the full text of documents.

5.18   POLIS

POLIS - the Parliamentary On-Line Information System - is an index (and so not full text) to proceedings in Parliament. It indexes all House of Commons and House of Lords Bills since May 1979 and November 1981 respectively and debates on legislation since November 1982.

5.19   DIALOG

The Legal Resources Index which covers journal articles published in the UK and USA can be accessed through the DIALOG database which also includes social science and education indexes.

5.20   End of chapter references and additional reading

Butterworth Telepublishing   *How to Use LEXIS*

Butterworth Telepublishing   *What is LEXIS*

Mead Data Central   *The LEXIS Service for Law Students
                                Training Workbook*

Butterworth Telepublishing   *LEXIS Library Contents and Price
(1992)   List April 1992*

Context Ltd   *JUSTIS User Manual
(1992)   Version 4.3*

Appendix I

Non-searchable words on LEXIS

all   any
also   are
am   as
an   at
and

be   been
because

could

did   do
does

eg   ever

from

had   hereby
hardly   herein
has   hereof
have   hereon
having   hereto
he   herewith
hence   him
her   his
here   however

ie   is
if   it
into   its

me

nor

of	or
on	our
onto	

really

said	so
she	some
should	such

the	thereof
their	thereon
them	thereto
than	therewith
that	these
then	they
there	this
thereby	those
therefore	thus
therefrom	to
therein	too

unto	us

very	viz

was	whether
we	which
were	who
what	whom
when	whose
where	why
whereby	with
wherein	would

you

CHAPTER

6 Evaluation and Presentation of Research Findings

'True ease in writing comes from art, not chance,
As those move easiest who have learn'd to dance'.

Alexander Pope (1688-1744)

6.1 What next?

You have now completed the initial legal information retrieval stage of your research. However, do not be tempted at this stage to dive in and start to draft your final product. You must first organise and evaluate the information gathered. This evaluation may suggest that further fact-finding is necessary and that may, in turn, give rise to the necessity for further investigation. Once this process is complete, your next objective is to present the product of your research in an effective and appropriate way.

Effective presentation depends very much, of course, on your (or your secretary's) ability to write English which is, in the first place, technically correct. Software is now available which will check both spelling and grammar and which will identify uses of English which do not accord with the accepted conventions. Do not undervalue the skill of using English properly. Your future clients may not be able to assess you on your legal knowledge but they will form an impression of you based on your ability to communicate, both in writing and orally. Poor use of English can also lead to confusion and ambiguity.

Important as this skill is, however, it is not the purpose of this chapter to review the technical or stylistic dimensions of your written English. Instruction on legal writing is given in another of the texts in this series ('Legal Writing' by Margot Costanzo). Instead, this chapter suggests an approach which may assist you in structuring the presentation of your research findings.

This chapter will propose:

- that you review the usefulness of information gathered from your research by asking a series of evaluative questions (suggested below at para 6.2)

- that you consider the factors which will influence the form and/ or character of the presentation of your research findings

- that you apply a systematic technique for structuring the presentation of your research findings.

6.2   Evaluation of research findings

Once you have completed the process of information gathering, you will need to evaluate the extent to which the product of your research assists you in formulating an answer to your client's problem. The problem may be common and the answer clear. However, it may be that, although you have located relevant authority on a similar fact situation, material differences can be identified. You will need to assess the strength of your client's case and advise accordingly. What if you have been unable to identify any authority which appears to be directly relevant?

The following questions will assist you in evaluating the usefulness of your research findings. Many of the cases used to illustrate the principles will be familiar to you, although you may not have used them in the present context.

1   What are the material facts of the problem you are trying to solve and how, if at all, do they differ from the previous authorities you have identified?

You will have learned in your undergraduate studies that the ratio of a case is found by application of the appropriate rule of law to the material facts of the case. You will have come across many instances where judges have chosen to distinguish a later case from an earlier decision on the facts. The importance of identifying what the material facts of any case are should be obvious. If you wish to rely on a previous authority to support your client's claim, you will wish to draw as close an analogy as possible between the fact situations. If previous authority does not support your client's claim, you will wish to draw material distinctions between the cases.

You may have received informal instruction on material fact extraction and analysis at undergraduate level. If you have not received formal instruction, you will certainly have engaged in such activity when reading and analysing cases - in particular, if you have participated in mooting. However, it may be useful to review the process quickly here.

You will be familiar with the case of *Donoghue v Stevenson*. Here, the precise material facts may have been extracted immediately after the decision as follows:

- bottle of ginger-beer
- bought by A, consumed by B
- bottle opaque
- bottle sealed
- bottle contained remains of decomposed snail
- consumer suffered gastro-enteritis and nervous shock

Of course, these material facts are stated in a very specific way and, were we to restrict the application of the principle formulated in *Donoghue v Stevenson* to these precise facts, its application would be unduly limited to cases of decomposed snails in opaque and sealed bottles of ginger-beer etc. But at what level of generality should the facts be defined, thus extending (or restricting) the application of the principle?

6.2.1   Exercise One

Before you read further, spend 5 minutes analysing the above list and re-define each of the terms to reflect what you consider to be the essential *characteristic* of each of the terms in context. For example, 'bottle of ginger beer' may be re-defined as 'drink', 'food' or 'product'. (This type of exercise is also useful in generating search terms.)

You may have generated a list similar to the following with progressive levels of generality:

ginger-beer	drink food something for internal consumption product
consumer	user
opaque	preventing visual inspection
sealed	non-examinable condition unchanged since leaving manufacturer
decomposed snail	noxious/poisonous harmful substance
gastro-enteritis and nervous shock	physical and mental illness physical or mental illness injury

As a result of this process, we *might* argue that the principle of law in *Donoghue v Stevenson* as at 1932 applied to fact situations where someone suffered injury as a consequence of using a product which contained a latent defect due to negligence in manufacture.

Similarly, the principle of law in *Donoghue v Stevenson* is itself open to interpretation so enabling further extensions or limitations to be argued. Some of these have, of course, been determined by the courts. For example, whether the neighbour principle applies to cases of exclusively nervous shock (and what constitutes such: see *Hinz v Berry* [1970] 2 QB 40 CA); the limitations on the application of the principle to be applied in such cases (see *McLoughlin v O'Brian* [1983] AC 410 HL; *Alcock v Chief Constable of South Yorkshire Police* [1991] 3 WLR 1057 HL; *Ravenscroft v Rederiaktiebolaget Transatlantic* [1992] 2 All ER 470 CA); whether the principle applies to cases of economic loss (see *Hedley Byrne & Co v Heller and Partners* [1964] AC 465). As shown by the *Alcock* case, the courts are still engaged in defining the limits of the principle in its application to developments in technology not foreseen in 1932 (here the simultaneous transmission of the Hillsborough football stadium disaster on TV).

2   Can you identify any ambiguity, uncertainty or vagueness in the case-law or statutory provision which would assist your argument?

Language is, by its nature, ambiguous. The meaning of an oral statement can change according to inflexion, tone or even demeanour, none of which you have to assist you when interpreting the intended meanings of the judge or Parliamentary draftsperson. Despite the attempted precision and detail of the Parliamentary draftsperson in formulating statutes, ambiguities cannot be eradicated. On the other hand, treaty obligations are often drafted in deliberately vague terms - so much so that, on occasions, British judges have felt unable to determine their intended meaning (see, for example, the references to Article 8 of the European Convention on Human Rights made by Sir Robert Megarry VC in *Malone v Metropolitan Police Commissioner* [1979] Ch 344). This, of course, has been a particular problem with EC treaty obligations and served to justify the existence of the referral procedure under Art 177 of the Treaty of Rome for preliminary rulings on questions of interpretation or validity of EC law (see, for example, the case of *Factortame v Secretary of State for Transport* [1989] 2 All ER 692 HL).

6.2.2   Exercise Two

Spend 10 minutes examining each of the following extracts from case-law, statute and treaty for ambiguity or uncertainty, and answer the questions posed.

<u>Example 1</u>

Ghani v Jones [1970] 1 QB 693 at p 706 per Lord Denning MR:

> *'I would start by considering the law where police officers enter a man's house by virtue of a warrant, or arrest a man lawfully, with or without a warrant, for a serious offence. I take it to be settled law, without citing cases, that the officers are entitled to take any goods which they find in his possession or in his house which they reasonably believe to be material evidence in relation to the crime for which he is arrested or for which they enter.'*

Applying this statement of Lord Denning, in which of the following situations would the search of the person or premises and seizure of goods by the police have been lawful? (NB *Ghani v Jones* is not, of course, a statement of the current law on police powers of search and seizure. See now the Police and Criminal Evidence Act 1984 ss 18 and 19.)

i)   Stan was arrested without a warrant for drugs offences. The police searched him and found cannabis in his jacket pocket.

Would your answer differ if Stan had been arrested for being drunk and disorderly?

ii)   Stan was arrested in Holborn for drugs offences. The police, without a warrant, searched his home in the Barbican and found stolen goods.

Would your answer differ if the police had obtained a warrant to search for drugs?

In this example, ambiguity or confusion arises from a lack of definition of the term 'serious offence' and an attempt to deal with at least two concepts - search of the person and seizure of goods upon arrest and search of premises and seizure of goods in pursuance of a search warrant - simultaneously. Lord Denning's statement may have been interpreted in any one of the following ways:

i)   that where police officers enter a man's house by virtue of a warrant, the officers are entitled to take any goods which they find in his house which they reasonably believe are material evidence in relation to the crime for which they enter;

ii)   that where police officers arrest a man lawfully, with or without a warrant, for a serious offence, they are entitled to take any goods which they find in his possession which they reasonably believe are material evidence in relation to the crime for which he is arrested;

iii) that where police officers arrest a man lawfully, with or without a warrant, for a serious offence, they are entitled to take any goods which they find in his house (thus presupposing legality of a search of the house) which they reasonably believe to be material evidence in relation to the crime for which he is arrested.

The third of these propositions was the most contentious and subsequently became the subject of judicial consideration in the case of *Jeffrey v Black* [1978] QB 490.

In the above example, what research might you have undertaken to assist you in clarifying Lord Denning's statement?

Example 2

S 1(1) of the Guard Dogs Act 1975 provides:

'A person shall not use or permit the use of a guard dog at any premises unless a person ('the handler') who is capable of controlling the dog is present on the premises and the dog is under the control of the handler at all times while it is being so used except while it is secured so that it is not at liberty to go freely about the premises.'

Applying this section, in which of the following situations would the conduct of the defendant, Joe, who keeps three guard dogs on his premises, be unlawful under the Act? The premises consist of a scrap metal yard which is kept locked and a small workshop.

i)   When Joe was in the workshop the dogs would be tied to chains which allowed them to roam freely about the yard;

ii)   When Joe was not on the premises, his security guard, Pete, was. Pete allowed the dogs to roam freely about the yard at all times when he was on the premises;

iii)   Pete would secure the dogs on the chains if he left the premises at any time;

iv)   The dogs would be secured at all times;

v)   Pete does not always feel like working throughout the night. On these occasions, Pete secures the dogs and leaves his nephew, Tom, in charge of the premises. Tom cannot control the dogs.

Would your answers differ if the premises consisted of a car repair workshop and yard open to the public from 9-6 Monday to Saturday?

Would your answer to (v) differ if Joe was unaware of Pete's arrangement with Tom?

Are there any further facts you need to know?

In this example, the ambiguity or confusion arises from the use of an over-long sentence by the draftsperson and a consequent lack of clarity about the relationship between component parts of the section. It is unclear to what situations the exception is intended to apply. The section may have been interpreted in the following ways:

i)   that whenever a guard dog is used, a handler must be present with the dog under his control. If the handler is not present and in control, the dog must be secured;

ii)   a handler need not be present so long as he is somewhere on the premises;

iii)   a handler need not be on the premises at all, provided the dog is secured.

A further ambiguity arises from a lack of definition of the phrase 'liberty to go freely' or the failure to use more precise language. In the above example, would a dog have the liberty to go freely if attached to a chain but the chain was of such a length as to allow the dog access to all parts of the premises? Would it make any difference if the dog could be denied access to the workshop by shutting the workshop door? Would it make any difference if the dog could access the entire premises except for a space of two feet around the perimeter?

What principles of construction might assist you in interpreting s1(1) of the 1975 Act?

How would you begin to research this problem if you had only a bare statement of the facts? Having discovered the relevant provision of the Guard Dogs Act, how would you locate relevant case-law?

Your research should lead you to the case of *Hobson v Gledhill* [1978] 1 WLR 215, an appeal to the Divisional Court by case stated.

Before you go any further, read the judgments in *Hobson v Gledhill*. Ask yourself:

- To what extent do these resolve the ambiguity and provide answers to the above situations?
- To what extent does the Act remain unclear?
- What were the objectives of the Act?
- How would you discover those objectives?
- Are they fully achieved in *Hobson v Gledhill*?

Example 3

S 1(2)(a) of the Equal Pay Act 1970 provides for an equality clause to be included in a woman's contract of employment where 'the woman is employed on like work with a man in the same employment'.

Article 119 of the Treaty of Rome provides:

'Each Member State shall during the first stage ensure and subsequently maintain the application of the principle that men and women should receive equal pay for equal work...'

Article 8 of the European Convention on Human Rights protects the right, inter alia, to a 'private life' and Article 14 prohibits discrimination on the grounds, inter alia, of sex or association with a minority.

Applying each of these provisions, in which of the following situations involving Jane and Fred might the discriminatory conduct practised be unlawful?

i)   Jane is employed as a secretary in a Job Centre. She is paid £3.00 per hour. Fred, the cleaner, is paid £3.75 per hour;

ii)   On Fred's retirement, Jane applies for the post of cleaner. She is appointed but is disappointed to learn that she is to be paid £3.25 per hour;

iii)   Jane discloses to her employers that she is a transsexual and was born 'John'. Her pay, however, remains unchanged;

iv)   Jane knows that the relief cleaner, Mabel, who works when Jane is on holiday or sick, is paid £3.50 per hour and that Mabel's brother, Bill, who works as cleaner at another branch of the Job Centre, is paid £3.40 an hour.

A number of problems of construction of both the statute and the treaties are raised here, as well as the relationship between the relevant municipal law and the respective treaties.

* Do the provisions of the Equal Pay Act and Article 119 permit comparison with a predecessor in the same employment?

* Can comparisons be made between employees based at different locations?

* When is work 'equal' or 'like'?

- Can a man use the Equal Pay Act if his terms and conditions of employment are less advantageous than those of comparable women?

- How is a person's sex to be defined for the purposes of the Act or the treaties?

Research this problem and formulate an answer to each of the four questions posed above.

The importance of these exercises for present purposes is to illustrate the importance of analysis and evaluation of your research findings. You will be seeking to identify an interpretation of existing law which is most favourable to your client's case. If you can identify a lack of clarity in the existing law, you will need to evaluate how likely it is that the interpretation most supportive of your client will succeed.

It may be that the ambiguity or lack of clarity arises by virtue of the existence of a provision of EC law or an article of the European Convention on Human Rights. In such a case, you must be clear on the relationship between law emanating from the EC institutions and that from the UK Parliament and also the relationship between the European Convention (and other international treaties which have not been embodied in statute) and UK law. You must also be familiar with the procedure under Article 177 for declarations by the European Court on the interpretation or validity of EC law and with the procedure for complaint at an international level to the European Commission on Human Rights for alleged breaches of the European Convention.

3   Does the context of the statutory provision assist your argument for its application/ non-application to the problem?

There may be several 'contexts' to be considered here. One is the meaning of the words to be interpreted in the context of the words immediately surrounding them or in the context of the Act as a whole. The context of the Act itself may be derived from, for

example, Parliamentary debates on the introducton of the Bill or
the reports of Royal Commissions preceding such introduction.
Hansard can now, of course, be used by the courts as an aid to
the construction of legislation which is ambiguous or obscure or
the literal meaning of which leads to absurdity - if the reference
discloses the mischief aimed at or the legislative intention lying
behind the ambiguity or obscurity. See *Pepper (Inspector of
Taxes) v Hart and Others* [1992] 3 WLR 1032.

If the Act is a consolidating Act, then judicial interpretations of
equivalent provisions under the preceding legislation must also
be identified.

4 Can analogies be drawn with the interpretation of other similar statutory provisions or other case-law?

On occasions, analogies are usefully drawn with the meaning of the
same or similar words in other legislation. For example, Schedule 1,
Part I, paragraph 5 of the Mobile Homes Act 1983 states:

> *'The owner (of a mobile home site) shall be entitled to
> terminate the agreement forthwith if, on the application of
> the owner, the court is satisfied that the occupier is not
> occupying the mobile home as his only or main residence.'*

In the recent case of *Omar Parks v Elkington* (1993) 65 P &
CR 26 the Court of Appeal had to determine, in an application by
a site owner to terminate an agreement with a mobile home
owner, whether occupation of the mobile home under this
provision was to be judged at the time of the application to the
court or at the time of the actual hearing.

The provision was ambiguous and the court was confronted
with conflicting decisions of the County Court. In interpreting the
provision, the Court of Appeal looked to the established
interpretation of similar provisions in the Rent Acts and the
Landlord and Tenant Act 1954. It concluded that occupation was
to be judged at the date of the hearing rather than the date of the
application to court.

5 Are there any policy issues to be considered in determining whether the principle of law to be argued should be confined, restricted further, or extended?

You will have come across numerous cases where policy considerations - implicitly or explicitly - have influenced, or even determined, the outcome of a case. The law of tort is rife with such cases. One example is *Home Office v Dorset Yacht Co* [1970] AC 1004, where the House of Lords was not persuaded by the argument that the duty of care should be excluded for reasons of public policy, ie that the existence of such a duty would affect the way in which penal institutions would perform their statutory duties and inhibit innovation in dealing with offenders. See also *Alcock v Chief Constable of South Yorkshire Police* (above) where the House of Lords appeared anxious not to open the floodgates to claimants in nervous shock cases. Difficulty of enforcement may be another influence. In *Paton v Trustees of the British Pregnancy Advisory Service* [1978] 2 All ER 987 where a husband applied for an injunction to prevent his wife having an abortion, Sir George Baker, in refusing the application, could not envisage that imprisonment for breach of a court order would be a viable option in such circumstances. Such policy influences may not always be explicitly stated.

6 Is the existing state of the law under pressure for reform?

At a strictly constitutional level, judges in the United Kingdom have little scope for being innovative or responsive to demands for innovation or change in the law. Their constitutional function, in the absence of a written constitution or a bill of rights, is to interpret the law. Within this constitutional framework, it might be argued that it is more appropriate for the legislature than the judiciary to intervene and effect change demanded by the prevailing mood of the public. Indeed, this view is often voiced by judges themselves. However, we all know that the interpretative function itself gives the judges considerable scope for manoeuvre and that the common law is subject to judicial revision.

There are undoubtedly instances of judicial decision-making being responsive to public opinion. A recent example is to be found in the cases on marital rape and, in particular, *Reg* v *R* [1991] 2 WLR 1065. Here the Court of Appeal concluded that the contention that a husband could not be guilty of a rape on his wife, as pronounced by Sir Matthew Hale in his 'History of the Pleas of the Crown' (1736) and reaffirmed in the first edition of Archbold (1822), was no longer good law. Lord Lane CJ considered that the exceptions which the courts had since developed to Hale's principle were 'a legitimate use of the flexibility of the common law which can and should adapt itself to changing social attitudes' (at page 1073). Further, 'where the common law rule no longer even remotely represents what is the true position of a wife in present day society, the duty of the court is to take steps to alter the rule if it can legitimately do so in the light of any relevant Parliamentary enactment' (ibid). This the Court of Appeal felt itself able to do, overcoming the problem of statutory interpretation presented by the reference to '**unlawful** sexual intercourse' in section 1(1) of the Sexual Offences (Amendment) Act 1976. In reaching its decision, the court regarded the prior rule as a 'common law fiction' which had become 'anachronistic and offensive' (at page 1074).

6.3   Presentation of research findings

You are now at the stage when you are ready to prepare a draft of your research findings in response to the problem to be addressed. This may take the form of a written memorandum, an advice letter or possibly an oral presentation to your principal.

However good your understanding of the law and ability to apply it to the situation at hand, you must be able to present your product in the most cogent form appropriate to the task. Part of what we are concerned with here is a host of essentially literary skills which are all too often undervalued by law undergraduates. If you cannot express yourself articulately and effectively, the brilliance of your legal argument will be entirely lost on your audience (see *Legal Writing* by Margot Costanzo in this series).

In addition to the ability to write clearly, the effective presentation of your research findings depends on the structure and form chosen by you in which to 'package' your work. Here we shall consider some of the essential qualities of a good presentation which are equally important as literary ability.

Think of a production - a book, film, play, legal judgment - which has gained your attention. Analyse the qualities which have successfully attracted and kept your interest.

The list you generated might contain the following:

- plot
- structure *
- subject-matter
- players/characters
- individuality
- polish *
- clarity *
- use of language *
- description
- conciseness *
- relevance *
- treatment of subject-matter *

Of course, not all of these qualities will be of equal (or any) relevance to all pieces of writing, although those marked * will probably always be of relevance to a piece of legal writing. The nature of the presentation, the objective(s) it is hoped to achieve and the audience or reader(s) will all affect the form it takes.

6.3.1   What is the objective of your presentation/written product?

Written products or legal documents take many forms and have various objectives. These will influence the nature of the language used and, to an extent, the structure of the document. Your objective may, for example, be:

- to persuade
- to inform
- to record
- to threaten
- to sympathise
- to extract information
- to demand
- a combination of two or more of the above

You should take the time to determine both the general objective(s) of your presentation (for example, from the above list) and also the more specific objectives you wish to achieve in this particular case (for example, 'to persuade Ms X to settle her claim against Mr Y by accepting his offer rather than proceeding to litigation').

6.3.2   Who is the intended audience?

Similarly, the person for whom your product is intended - for example, whether the audience or reader is a lay person or a fellow lawyer - will influence both its language and structure.

6.3.3   Structure

Given the potential range of objectives and audiences for any one presentation or written product (see above), there is no one systematic technique for presenting your research findings. The presentation may take a variety of forms. Sometimes, the choice may be yours. More often, it will be dictated to you. It may be oral or written. If written, it may be in the form of a letter (advisory, persuasive or demanding), memorandum, legal opinion, brief etc. What is essential is that, once the form of the presentation is determined, you give deliberate thought to how the product of your research can be presented in the most effective manner.

One of the most common techniques for structuring information is the IRAC - issue, rule, application, conclusion - formula. This can be a useful formula to assist in the structuring of written memoranda, letters of advice and so on. It follows this format:

Issue

State the issue(s) of fact and/or law which need to be answered.

Rule

State the rule(s) of law, with authority, which are relevant to each of the issues raised.

Application

Apply the rule(s) as stated to the issue(s) identified.

Conclusion

Conclude your findings on each of the issues raised and identify areas where the conclusion is unclear (stating why) or which need further investigation of the facts and/or law.

This model may, of course, be adapted and experimented with according to the form of your presentation. A memorandum or letter, for example, may be more appropriately structured as follows:

Formalities (for example, in a memo, 'to' 'from' 'date' 'subject')

Facts

Issue(s)

Relevant law and application

Conclusion(s) and recommendations

Discussion of, for example, areas which remain problemmatic or unclear or where further action is considered necessary.

Both the IRAC formula and this derivative may, of course, be further adapted according to the objective of your presentation and the needs of your audience.

6.3.4   Exercise Three

Consider the following example of the use of the IRAC formula.

Facts

Your client, Mrs Dee, was employed recently as assistant to the Personnel Officer in a small employment agency. The Personnel Officer gave her a list of employers who are not prepared to consider non-white applicants for managerial posts. Mrs Dee does not approve of this. However, she does not want to lose her job by complaining or refusing to comply with an instruction to tell applicants in these cases that vacancies have been filled.

Consider researching the law relevant to this situation and try to structure a memorandum to your principal advising her of your client's case. Compare your product with the sample below.

Issue 1

Is the employer acting unlawfully by instructing Mrs Dee to discriminate against persons of colour?

Rule 1

Section 30 of the Race Relations Act 1976 makes it an offence to instruct a person to discriminate on racial grounds. Section 30 is enforceable only by the Commission for Racial Equality issuing proceedings under s 63 in the County Court.

Application

The Personnel Officer is acting in contravention of s 30 of the 1976 Act in instructing Mrs Dee to discriminate. The fact that he may not be motivated by a personal desire to discriminate but by pressure from his clients is irrelevant (see *R v CRE ex parte Westminster City Council* [1985] ICR 827 CA). However, she cannot institute proceedings under s 30. The Commission for Racial Equality could issue proceedings under s 63 were it to be informed of the discriminatory instruction.

Issue 2

Will Mrs Dee be protected if she were to inform the CRE and was dismissed as a consequence?

Rule 2

Section 2 of the Act outlaws discrimination by way of victimisation. S 2(1)(d) protects a person who has been treated less favourably on the basis that the discriminator has committed an act which would amount to a contravention of the Act. However, if the information on which the allegation is based is received in confidence (for example, by way of employment) the employee can be dismissed lawfully for that breach of confidence (see *Kirby v Manpower Services Commission* [1980] ICR 420 EAT and *Aziz v Trinity Street Taxis Ltd* [1988] 534 CA).

Section 1(1)(a) of the Act makes it a civil offence to treat a person less favourably on racial grounds. 'Racial grounds' is defined in s 3 of the Act as meaning 'colour, race, nationality, or ethnic or national origins'. For s 1 to operate, a person need not be discriminated against on the ground of his or her own colour etc. It is sufficient if he or she is being discriminated against on the basis of someone else's colour etc (see *Showboat Entertainment Centre v Owens* [1984] 1 WLR 384 EAT). A person who is dismissed because he or she refuses to comply with an instruction to discriminate will be directly discriminated against under s 1(1)(a) (see *Zarczynska v Levy* [1979] ICR 184 EAT). The victim of the discrimination may issue proceedings under s 54 in the industrial tribunal. Employment generally is covered in Part II of the Act and dismissal from employment specifically in s 4(1)(c). The Act does not require a minimum period of employment before it operates to protect an employee.

Application

Mrs Dee could complain to the CRE in the hope that it would act under s 30. However, despite the protection afforded under s 2(1)(d) to persons treated less favourably for alleging that the discriminator has contravened the Act, it appears that she could, as an employee, be dismissed lawfully for breach of confidence (*Kirby v Manpower Services Commission* and *Aziz v Trinity Street Taxis Ltd*).

If Mrs Dee refused to comply with the instruction and was dismissed as a consequence, she would have been discriminated against on racial grounds under s 1(1)(a) of the 1976 Act (direct discrimination) (*Zarczynska v Levy*). This would apply even though she was not discriminated against on the ground of her own colour, but that of the potential applicants for the managerial posts (*Showboat Entertainment Centre v Owens*).

Conclusions and recommendations

Mrs Dee should be advised that it is not in her best interests to disclose her employer's instruction to the Commission for Racial Equality. She can, however, refuse to comply with the instruction and, if dismissed for this, she could bring an action in the industrial tribunal for compensation, including damages for injury to feelings. She would not, however, be entitled to reinstatement but the tribunal can make recommendations. Reinstatement can be awarded under s 69 of the Employment Protection (Consolidation) Act 1978 for unfair dismissal, but Mrs Dee does not fulfil the qualifying period of employment (2 years).

6.3.5   Preparing drafts

At least in the early stages of your traineeship, you should always make a draft of every document you are asked to prepare, however simple it might appear. Evaluate the draft. You will rarely find that you cannot improve upon it.

6.3.6 Pre-presentation checklist

Before commencing the final draft of your presentation, check the following list to gauge whether you are ready to proceed. You will very soon operate your own checklist without conscious reference to the list below.

- have you read any instructions and complied with them?
- do you know your client's goals?
- have you identified all the facts relevant to the problem?
- have you clearly identified the issue(s), legal and/or factual, which is (are) the focus of your presentation?
- have you completed all relevant research?
- do you understand the relevant law and its application to the relevant issue(s)? If necessary, have you sought further advice?
- have you identified the objectives of your presentation, for example, to inform, to persuade, to pacify, to threaten, to negotiate or to settle?
- have you considered the context of your presentation, for example, to whom it is to be presented, when, where, for how long?
- have you identified and evaluated alternative conclusions/recommendations?
- have you identified potential arguments for the opposing side? Do you have adequate responses?
- have you considered the overall structure of your presentation? Is it logical? Is it coherent? Is it progressive? Does it answer the issue addressed?
- have you prepared a draft/re-draft? If necessary, have you received comments on it?
- do you feel ready to commit yourself to writing the final product?

If the answer to each of these questions is 'yes', then you are now in a position to start writing your final product. Once your final draft is complete, however, **always remember to review and edit it carefully.** Ask, finally, does it meet your original objective or objectives?

6.4   End of chapter references and additional reading

Calleros, C   *Legal Method and Writing*
(1990)   Little, Brown & Co

Ramsfield, J   *Getting it Right and Getting it Written*
(1989)   West Publishing Co

CHAPTER

7 Conclusion

'Research! A mere excuse for idleness; it has never achieved, and will never achieve, any results of the slightest value.'

Benjamin Jowett (1877-98)

By now you will hopefully feel able to take intelligent issue with the above statement. The skill of legal research is central to the everyday work of the lawyer. The efficacy with which you deal with almost any practice task - whether it is a piece of legal writing or drafting, advocacy or a negotiation - will often depend directly on your research efforts.

This text was designed to introduce you to a three-stage model for legal research (i) planning for research (ii) implementation of a research plan and (iii) presentation of research findings. Your training in legal research is by no means complete, but you should now be on the road to becoming an effective legal researcher. You should be able to display competence in fulfilling the Law Society's written standards for legal research (see Chapter 1).

In particular, in a given problem situation you should be able to:

- extract relevant facts
- identify your own and your client's goal(s)
- find the law
- identify the relationship between the legal and factual situations
- up-date the law
- analyse the law
- identify and, so far as possible, fill factual omissions
- evaluate your findings from a legal and policy perspective
- if necessary, innovate
- present your findings in an effective and appropriate manner

The day will soon be upon you when you no longer have a tutor to inform and advise you. You will have to take the initiative and assume responsibility for your own learning and for the products of your own work. If you have acquired effective research skills, you can be confident that your knowledge is accurate and up-to-date.

Many of the exercises in this text have been tested on students at Anglia *Polytechnic* University, in particular those LLB students who opted for the module on Research Skills introduced in October 1992. This text will end with a part of the exercise which formed the basis for assessment of that module and extracts from a sample student answer. Once again, you are invited to attempt the exercise and to compare your product with the sample answer provided.

MEMORANDUM

TO: Trainee   FROM: Principal
DATE: 1 December 1992   SUBJECT: Assignment

You will find below a note of an interview conducted by myself on 27 November 1992. Please conduct the necessary research and present your findings (500-750 words) to me by 11 December.

INTERVIEW NOTE

DATE: 27 November 1992
CLIENT: Mrs Valerie Scott
ADDRESS: 18 Bolton Road, Hebden Bridge, West Yorks
           HB1 1CD
TEL: 0422-555555

Client 45 years old. Married twice with three children. Eldest child, Tom, by her first husband. Tom aged 18 and at university. Other children by second husband, Victor. Twins, Danny and Julia, aged 7. Family unit very close. Twins had exceptionally close relationship and spent most of their time together.

14 January 1992 - Danny and Julia in school mini-bus when it collided with lorry. Accident allegedly due to negligence of mini-bus driver who has since been prosecuted and convicted. Client not clear of charge.

On day of accident, client at work. Husband contacted at home by police and informed of accident. Husband was advised that Danny in serious condition. Tried to contact Mrs S but failed. Husband went to hospital and saw Danny. Injuries very extensive.

Husband phoned Mrs S from hospital. Told her Danny involved in accident and to come. She left immediately but Danny had died before she arrived. Victor advised her not to see Danny's body. She agreed.

Mrs S has since suffered severe depression. Regrets not having seen Danny after death. Diagnosed as having post-traumatic stress. Julia very withdrawn and under medical supervision. Advise.

Follow-up interview: 14 December 1992 at 2.00 pm. Please attend.

RESEARCH PLAN

1 Analyse the facts

PARTIES

- Mrs Scott, mother of Danny, victim of post-traumatic stress
- Julia, twin of Danny, minor, victim of minor injuries and (?) nervous shock
- Driver of school mini-bus
- Education authority or school as driver's employer?

PLACES

- No facts
- Was driver on authorised route?
- Was driver speeding?

OBJECTS

- State of mini-bus. Roadworthy?
- Relationships in family - close - twins - mother and death of young child
- Hospital - usual practice on viewing deceased? - advice sought?
- Medical reports on (i) Mrs Scott (ii) Julia? Prognosis?

BASIS

- Tort of negligence
- Duty of care of driver/employer to children as passengers and to parents - breach of duty - damage
- Foreseeability, causation, remoteness
- Physical injury (Julia), nervous shock (Mrs S and Julia)
- Proximity of (i) relationships (ii) perception in space and time

DEFENCE

- Mrs S's post-traumatic stress:

  i)   *novus actus interveniens* (Mr S)?

  ii) proximity of perception?

  iii) *volenti non fit injuria*?

- Julia's physical injuries: no defence

- Julia's nervous shock: medical evidence (*prima facie* proximity of relationship but query 'aftermath')

RELIEF

- Objects not stated

- Damages? Quantum?

2 Formulate three preliminary issue statements

- UNDER the tort of negligence

  DID Mrs Scott and/or Julia suffer psychiatric illness for which D can be found liable

  WHEN D caused the accident which killed Danny?

- UNDER the tort of negligence

  DID Mr Scott's advice:

  i)   constitute a *novus actus interveniens* or

  ii) create a defence of *volenti non fit injuria* or

  iii) result in perception lacking on the part of Mrs Scott

  WHEN he advised her not to see Danny's body and she agreed?

- UNDER any statutory provision

  DID the driver's conviction become relevant

  WHEN Mrs Scott decided to consider civil proceedings?

3 Formulate research questions

- What is the recent case-law in 'nervous shock' cases, in particular post-Hillsborough, re:

  i) medical evidence

  ii) proximity of personal relationship in time, space, and medium of communication

  iii) policy and 'floodgates'?

- What is the current position re defences and limitation periods?

- What is the likely quantum of damages?

4 Formulate search terms for library-based research

- Negligence - nervous shock - psychiatric illness
- Damages - fatal accidents - personal injury - shock
- Evidence (convictions) and Negligence (defences)
- Limitation periods

5 Formulate search term(s) for LEXIS

- *Ravenscroft* or *Alcock* and date aft 1990

6 Search plan

Cases

- Latest edition of text to review area
- Current Law Monthly Digest for 1992 to up-date from Hillsborough
- Daily Law Reports Index for very recent cases

Articles

- Legal Journals Index by case and subject for post-1986 materials
- Latest Current Law Monthly Digests to up-date
- Contents pages of individual journals to up-date

Statutes

- Latest edition of text to review area
- Is It In Force? to check status
- Current Law Legislation Citators and latest Monthly Digest cumulative citator for judicial history and up-date

Other

- Judicial Office of the House of Lords to check whether *Ravenscroft* going to Lords on appeal
- Civil Appeal Office to check whether *Hevican v Ruane* going to Court of Appeal
- LEXIS for unreported cases

MEMORANDUM

TO: Principal   FROM: Trainee
DATE: 11 December 1992   SUBJECT: Mrs V. Scott
                                        Miss J Scott

Further to your memo dated 1 December, my findings in the above case are as follows:

1 PRELIMINARIES

1.1   Under the Limitation Act 1980, a 3 year time limit accrues from the date of the cause of action.

1.2   Further information is needed on the diagnosis of Julia and the prognosis for recovery of both Julia and Mrs Scott.

1.3   The Fatal Accidents Act 1976 section 1A as substituted by the Administration of Justice Act 1982 section 3 provides for compensation in cases of such bereavement.

1.4   Under the Civil Evidence Act 1968 section 11 the conviction of the driver can be pleaded in a civil suit for negligence.

2 THE CLAIMS

2.1   The facts are similar to *Hevican v Ruane* [1991] 3 All ER 65 and *Ravenscroft v Rederiaktiebolaget Transatlantic* [1991] 3 All ER 73.

2.3   In these cases, the plaintiffs neither saw nor heard the accidents in which their sons were killed, nor were they involved in the immediate aftermath. Both plaintiffs developed psychiatric illness. In both cases it was held that the chain of causation was established and the test was reasonable foreseeability of a risk of some kind of psychiatric damage. That the extent of the damage was not foreseeable was irrelevant.

2.4   Unfortunately, *Ravenscroft* was reversed on appeal (CA) [1992] 2 All ER 470. *Hevican* was listed for the CA but was settled out of court. Both first instance decisions were doubted by the HL in *Alcock v Chief Constable of South Yorks* [1991] 3 WLR 1057. The Judicial Office of the House of Lords had (as at 8.12.92) no notice of *Ravenscroft* being appealed further.

2.5 The CA in *Ravenscroft* held that statements made by their Lordships in *Alcock* that, for a defendant to be liable to a plaintiff for nervous shock, the shock had to come through sight or hearing of the relevant event or its aftermath were not obiter but 'an essential part of their Lordships' case'.

2.6 Mrs Scott, while proximate in relationship as a mother, is not proximate in time or space to the accident or its aftermath (unlike the plaintiff in *McLoughlin v O'Brian* [1983] AC 410 HL who saw the results of the accident).

2.7 It seems also that the act of Mr Scott could be seen as a *novus actus interveniens* if the cause of Mrs Scott's post-traumatic stress was not seeing her son's body.

2.8 In *Alcock*, Lord Ackner identified four relevant situations where liability would not arise despite foreseeability:

- if the injury is not induced by the shock but, for example, by the experience of coping with the loss of a loved one

- if the claimant is merely informed of or reads or hears about the accident

- if the suffering is mental, unaccompanied by any physical injury

- 'shock in this cause of action involves the sudden appreciation by sight or sound of a horrifying event which violently agitates the mind; it has yet to include psychiatric illness caused by the accumulation over a period of time of more gradual assaults on the nervous system'.

3 CONCLUSIONS

3.1 Mrs Scott is proximate in relationship and has suffered post-traumatic stress. However, in view of the HL decision in *Alcock* (compared with the judgment of Lord Bridge in *McLoughlin*) she is not proximate in 'seeing or hearing of the relevant event or its immediate aftermath'. She is unlikely to succeed in an action for damages in negligence. However, she and Mr Scott can claim £7,500 (as from 1 April 1991) under section 1A of the Fatal Accidents Act 1976, to be divided equally between them.

3.2   Julia was involved in the accident and is proximate. In *Turbyfield v Great Western Railway* (1937) 54 TLR 222, a twin witnessed her twin sister's accident and 'shock' damages were awarded. This must be viewed in the light of *Alcock*. Julia has sustained physical injuries for which she can claim. Details of her injuries are needed to assess quantum. Further information is required on her psychiatric condition, its causes, effect and the prognosis for recovery.

Useful Addresses

Butterworths Bookshop
9-12 Bell Yard
Temple Bar
London WC2A 2LF
Tel: 071 405 6900
Fax: 071 831 8922

Butterworth (Telepublishing) Ltd
LEXIS Customer Services
6 Bell Yard
London WC2A 2JR
Tel: 071 404 4097
Fax: 071 831 1463

Also at:

4 Hill Street
Edinburgh EH2 3JZ
Tel: 031 225 7828
Fax: 031 220 1833

Context Ltd
Tranley House
Tranley Mews
Fleet Road
London NW3 2QW
Tel: 071 267 7055
Fax: 071 267 2745

(Context Ltd produces the JUSTICE legal databases on CD-ROM)

Income Data Services Ltd
193 St John Street
London EC1V 4LS
Tel: 071 250 3434
Fax: 071 608 0949

(Income Data Services Ltd publishes the IDS Brief, handbooks, supplements and research reports on Employment Law)

Institute of Advanced Legal Studies
University of London
17 Russell Square
London WC1B 5DR
Tel: 071 637 1731
Fax: 071 436 8824

(Institute of Advanced Legal Studies has library facilities available to postgraduate students)

The Law Society
113 Chancery Lane
London WC2 1PL
Tel: 071 242 1222
Fax: 071 831 0344

Legal Information Resources Ltd
Rodmer Clough
Blackshawhead
West Yorkshire HX7 7PJ
Tel: 0422 886277
Fax: 0422 886250

(Legal Information Resources Ltd publishes inter alia manuals on legal research)

Society for Computers and Law
10 Hurle Crescent
Clifton
Bristol BS8 2TA

Tel: 0272 237393
Fax: 0272 239305

Sweet & Maxwell Ltd
South Quay Plaza
183 Marsh Wall
London E14 9FT

Tel: 071 538 8686

Fax: 071 538 8625 (Editorial)
         071 538 9508 (Marketing)
         071 538 8626 (Production)

For subscriptions, orders and accounts:

c/o ITPS
Cheriton House
North Way
Andover
Hampshire SP10 5BE

Tel: 0264 332424
Fax: 0264 364418